WILDERNESS REGAINED

The Story of the Virginia Barrier Islands

Curtis J. Badger

Copyright © 2022 by Curtis J. Badger

All rights reserved.

First Edition | First Printing June 2021
First Edition published under ISBN 978-1-62806-317-2 (print | paperback)
Library of Congress Control Number 2021907769

Second Edition | First Printing October 2022
Second Edition published under ISBN 978-1-62806-359-2 (print | paperback)

Published by Salt Water Media
29 Broad Street, Suite 104
Berlin, MD 21811
www.saltwatermedia.com

Cover image: Myrtle Island with a view southwest toward Little Inlet and Smith Island, by Gordon Campbell
AtAltitudeGallery.com
Used with permission and proper licensing

Interior map by Bill Nelson Cartography

To Dr. Brooks Miles Barnes
Who has cast a light on the Eastern Shore's past,
So that all of us may see it more clearly.

As with many other of the island gunning and fishing clubs, a record of its activities and the incidents occurring there, through the years, would make most interesting reading if someone one would make the effort to write it.

- Ralph T. Whitelaw, *Virginia's Eastern Shore*, 1951, on the Wallops Island Club

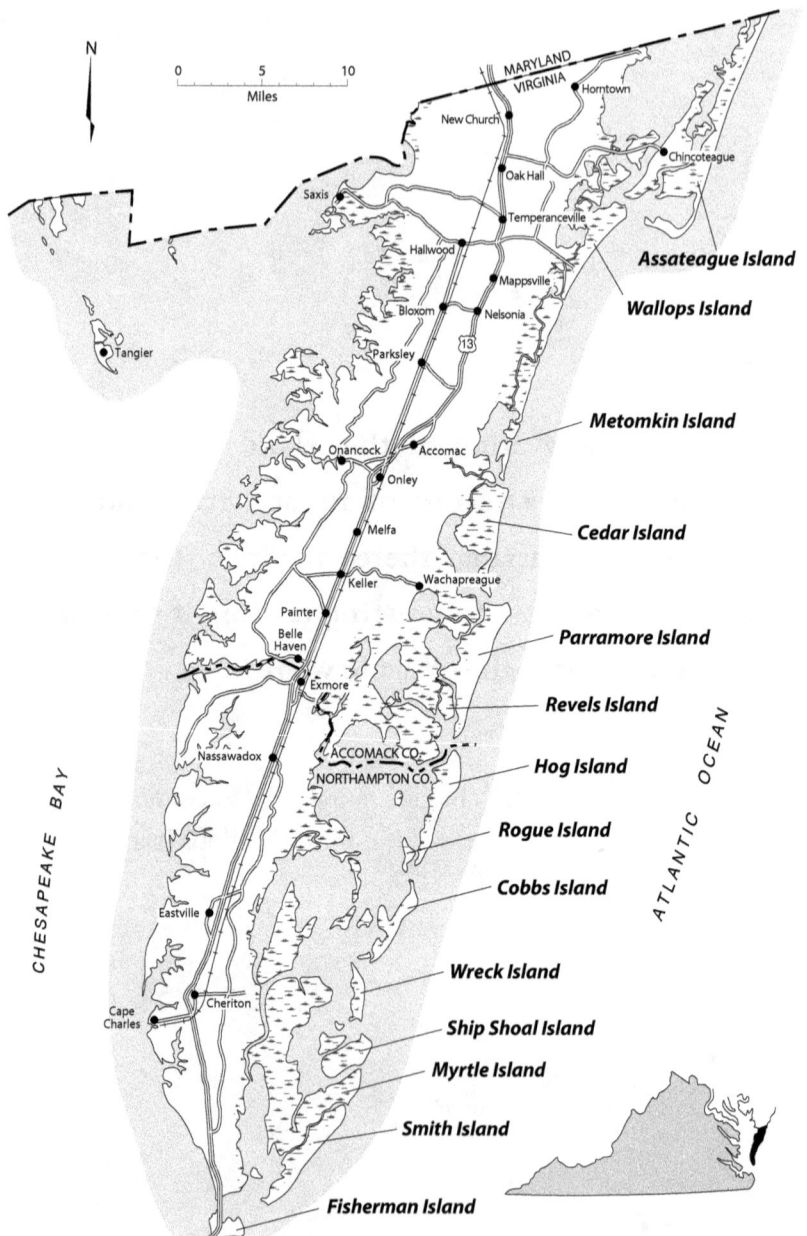

Contents

Author's Note to the Second Edition i

Wilderness Regained v

1. The Landscape 1
2. Past Presence 6
3. Assateague & Chincoteague Islands 14
4. Wallops Island 27
5. Cedar & Metompkin Islands 33
6. The Revels Island Club 40
7. The Accomac Club 52
8. Parramore Island 58
9. Hog Island 66
10. Broadwater Island 75
11. A Presidential Retreat 86
12. Nathan Cobb's Island 92
13. Mockhorn Island 103
14: Smith Island 108
15: Fisherman Island 113
16: The Life-Saving Stations & Coast Guard 122
17. Peninsulas in Repose — The Necks of the Eastern Shore 134
18. The Nature Conservancy 162

Bibliography 168

Index 173

Author's Note to the Second Edition

The wonderful thing about print-on-demand publishing is that it creates a book that is organic instead of static. That is, after the first print run, the text can easily be changed to add information not available during the first printing, errors can be corrected, and new research and details can be added.

In the months since *Wilderness Regained* was first published in July 2021, several important developments have come to light. It had long been believed that the Broadwater Club on Hog Island was a creation of Pennsylvania Railroad executives. It is true that many of the members were railroad men, but it turns out that the Broadwater Club was established by a couple from Germantown, Pennsylvania named Joseph and Elise Ferrell.

Joseph Ferrell was an engineer who did contract work for the railroad as it was being built on the Eastern Shore, and he realized that the railroad would make the pristine islands and beaches of the Shore easily accessible to people who lived in the population centers of the north. He and Elise went on a buying spree on Hog Island, and soon they were the majority landowner on the island. After the railroad opened in 1884, the Ferrells incorporated the Broadwater Land and Improvement Company to sell real estate on the island, and they built the Broadwater Club to attract wealthy members from northern cities. The term broadwater had been used in a generic sense to describe the marshy landscape that separates the mainland from the barrier islands, and the Ferrells took the name for their enterprise, reasoning that it would be much more marketable than the current name.

The Ferrells had a daughter named Mary-Russell, who spent her childhood on Hog Island while her parents went about the business of operating the Broadwater Club and selling vacation homes. Mary-Russell grew up to be a well-known artist and collector who focused on the American Southwest, and she and her husband, Harold Colton, founded the Museum of Northern Arizona in Flagstaff. The museum today has an extensive collection of Hopi and Navajo art, and it turns out that the museum collection also includes items from Mary-Russell's childhood days on Hog Island, giving us new insights into what was happening on Hog Island in the 1880s and 1890s.

It also came to light that one of the most famous restauranteurs of New York City during the mid-1800s was born the son of slaves on Chincoteague Island and began a career oystering in Chincoteague Bay. At the time of his death in 1866, Thomas Downing was known as the Oyster King of New York and was one of the city's wealthiest businessmen.

The major addition is Chapter 17, which is all about the necks of the Eastern Shore, a natural complement to our seaside islands and bayside beaches and marsh meadows. The English settled in wooded areas along the coast that were accessed by navigable creeks and streams, and as the population grew, wooded necks became the places where people chose to live. Necks became the original American community. The "neck of the woods" was your home.

Towns are a comparatively modern concept on the Eastern Shore, many a product of the railroad, which began rolling in 1884. Prior to the coming of the railroad, people lived and worked in the necks, and the creeks, bays, and inlets that surrounded the necks allowed travel and commerce with the wider world. Some forty named necks are in the two counties, and these are an important, and sometimes overlooked, aspect of Eastern Shore history.

Other additions are less ambitious, but they help round out the story of the human presence on the barrier islands. For example, there once was a plan to build a road linking Revels Island to the mainland. This came shortly after Custis Dunton in 1884 sold the island to a group of "northern capitalists" who established the Old Dominion Gunning and Angling Association, which later abridged its name to the Revels Island Club.

Chincoteague is famous for its annual pony penning celebration each summer, but ponies were rounded up on most of the islands, as were cattle, sheep, goats, hogs, and other valuable livestock. Parramore Island had two pony pennings in 1890, one in September and another in February. Animals grazed freely on the islands, and the roundups were part of the business of raising livestock.

One of the most important aspects of life on the barrier islands was the United States Life-Saving Service. Life-saving stations were first built on the islands in 1875, and they, and later coast guard stations, were part of the landscape for a century. They also contributed much to the drama and heroism of barrier island life. Only a few remnants of that era are with us today, but the stories of the life-saving crews demonstrate what a courageous and dedicated group of men once populated our islands. Of the many accounts of heroic action by members of the life-saving service, I have added the story of the *San Albano*, a Spanish ship that wrecked on Hog Island in 1892 with a crew of 27 sailors. The life-saving crew saved all but one man, and their heroic effort was rewarded with medals given by the King of Spain.

WILDERNESS REGAINED

Virginia's barrier islands are said to comprise the last stretch of wilderness along the unglaciated coast, which extends roughly from northern New Jersey to southern Georgia. Indeed, eighteen islands stretch for some one hundred miles along the seaside, a thin barrier of sand, shallow bays, wandering creeks, and great meadows of spartina grass. Other than a national seashore on Assateague and a NASA launch facility on Wallops, the islands now are as they may have been when Native Americans came to gather clams and oysters, or when the first blue-eyed British dandy stepped out of his dinghy and sank up to his crotch in marsh mud.

The barrier islands elsewhere on America's east coast have been extensively developed, from New Jersey south to the Outer Banks and along the sea islands of South Carolina and Georgia. In many cases, development has been so pervasive the islands no longer resemble islands, but a great assemblage of giant Lego blocks reaching for the sky, lined up precariously along an unseen ridge that separates the rolling ocean on the east from the shallow bays and spartina meadows on the west.

Along the Virginia coast there is little evidence that millions of people live less than a half-day drive away. The islands have no hotels, no bath houses, no restaurants, not even a road. To get there you come by boat, which is not always an easy task, given the shallow waters, the twisting channels, the constantly changing topography, and the capriciousness of the tides. But once there, you can walk a beach and see no other person, from horizon to horizon. The islands are emphatically wild places, as much so as a mountain range in the west or the tundra of Alaska.

That the Virginia barrier islands are described as wilderness, paradoxically, is a fairly recent phenomenon. Years ago, people lived here. Assateague had a village that centered around its lighthouse, and Hog Island at one time had a population of more than one hundred. There were stores and schools and churches. Most people lived in modest homes; there was little need for extravagance on a barrier island. The people's lives in those days were probably not unlike others in small communities across rural America. Folks worked, they grew and gathered food, they lived together as a society, worshipping together, sharing moments of plenty, and grieving together when the need arose.

The difference was that the people of the villages lived on islands, separated from the mainland by a substantial body of water, a barrier, some might assume, that made their lives different from the great majority of people, who lived on the mainland. But in the days of the island villages, water was not considered a barrier. It was, rather, a vital part of the infrastructure. It was how they traveled and worked, how they did business, how they explored the world around them.

Water did not become a barrier until the railroad came, followed soon after by the motor vehicle and the attendant highways and bridges. But before that happened, the world was connected by water. The barrier islands and mainland ports and docks were where business was done. The main spine of the Eastern Shore, the upland ridge, prior to the railroad, was rural and remote woodland.

The islands attracted commerce from all over the nation. The Cobb family from Eastham, Massachusetts, built a hotel on an island they bought in Northampton County, and from the time the Civil War ended until the 1890s it was one of the most famous beach resorts in America.

Just north of Cobb's Island is Hog Island, which had a substantial population in the 19th and early 20th centuries. They were a hardy group of people whose lives were closely connected to the land and to the sea that surrounded them.

The New York, Philadelphia and Norfolk (NYP&N) Railroad extended its line south through Virginia's Eastern Shore in 1884, and using a railroad barge to cross the Chesapeake Bay, established a link between the industrial north and the agricultural south. The opening of the railroad had a seismic impact on the landscape of the Eastern Shore, including the barrier islands.

Joseph and Elise Ferrell of Germantown, Pennsylvania bought large parcels of land on Hog Island and formed the Broadwater Land and Improvement Company, whose purpose was to sell vacation homes to wealthy northerners. The Ferrells constructed a hunting lodge called the Broadwater Club, whose membership consisted mainly of railroad executives. The club played host to president-elect Grover Cleveland before he began his second term in 1892. Cleveland spent nine days duck hunting on Hog Island, and his visit put the island, and its residents, in the national limelight for some two weeks. In addition to presidential visits, the Broadwater Club also served as the summer practice headquarters for the University of Pennsylvania football team in the late 1890s.

The railroad spurred development on other islands. A group of businessmen from New York built a lavish, members-only lodge on the marsh west of Parramore Island called the Accomac Club. Club members would take the NYP&N from New York to Keller, where they would catch a coach to Wachapreague and be transported by launch to the island. Many of the members of the Accomac Club were associated with the Fulton Fish Market in the city.

Revels Island, a vast inner marsh island south of Wachapreague, also had a members-only lodge, and several private residences were built on the island. George Shiras, a congressman from Pennsylvania, had a part time residence on the island for nearly forty years. Shiras was a well-known wildlife photographer and helped lay the groundwork for the Migratory Bird Treaty Act of 1918, which protected birds that nested on the marshes and beaches of the barrier islands.

A consortium of families from Pennsylvania bought Wallops Island and built a two-storied clubhouse in 1887. Incorporated as the Wallops Island Club, the group owned the island until the National Advisory Committee on Aeronautics, the forerunner of NASA, acquired the property through condemnation in 1945.

On the southern tip of the peninsula, Fisherman Island had a quarantine station where ships were required to stop so passengers could be screened for communicable diseases such as yellow fever and cholera. The first station opened in 1887 and operated through the World War I era. The military used the island to defend the capes during both world wars.

Most of the hotels and clubs on the islands lasted until the 1930s, although the venerable Cobbs Island resort succumbed to a coastal storm in 1896. Most were done in by a combination of rising tides and a sinking economy. The Great Depression took its toll on the membership clubs, and by the time the great hurricane of 1933 struck, the Accomac Club was down to five or six members.

The railroad had a profound effect on both the mainland and the barrier islands. The rail transformed the way farmers and fishermen marketed their goods, and it stimulated a period of growth and prosperity unlike anything previously experienced on the Eastern Shore. But like many changes that reach across economic and cultural divides, bad sometimes came with the good. The railroad brought growth to the islands, but it also turned the tradition of spring shorebird shooting into devastating slaughter that nearly wiped out many species of nesting and migrating birds. Local people had for years killed birds for the table, but when the railroad opened in 1884 spring shorebird shooting became popular among sportsmen from northern cities, and unregulated spring shooting endangered the populations of many species.

On the mainland, the railroad was like a great bonfire on a cold winter day; it drew people to it. As a result, people moved inland to enjoy the advantages of prosperous railroad communities such as Parksley.

For generations, my family lived on a farm on Red Bank Creek in

Northampton County, where they raised a variety of crops and engaged in a small shipping business. A few years after the railroad came, my grandfather left the creek and bought a farm in the community of Birdsnest. He built a two-storied frame farm house where he and my grandmother raised five children. You could stand on their front porch and see the trains pulling into Birdsnest station.

The railroad brought development to the islands as well as the mainland, as seafood was shipped to northern markets via rail links at Franklin City and Exmore. Driven by the railroad, the Eastern Shore enjoyed great prosperity in the first two decades of the twentieth century, and with that growing wealth came rapid advances in education, entertainment, travel, and health care. The Shore's first hospital, Northampton-Accomack Memorial, opened in Nassawadox in 1928.

The long-held view is that the islanders migrated to the mainland in the 1930s because of a rising sea level and frequent storms, but there also might have been more subtle issues. Islanders wanted better education for their children, and they wanted timely attention when they became injured, ill, or in need of extended care.

While our waterways had once been a link with the world, a part of the transportation infrastructure, it had become a barrier, and island residents had become isolated. Changes in transportation brought about changes in society. Once the Norwegian-American inventor Ole Evinrude perfected the outboard boat motor during the second decade of the twentieth century, it was no longer necessary to live in close proximity to where one fished.

Nonetheless, the tide was rising and everyone knew it. The islands were changing. Cobbs Island, one of America's great seaside resorts in the 1880s, was referred to as a sandbar in a newspaper article in the early 1900s. The Cobb family disinterred their loved ones, including their patriarch, and moved them from the island cemetery to one on the mainland. Coastal storms flattened dunes and flooded life-saving stations and hunting clubs. By the mid-1930s only the coast guardsmen were permanent residents, and by the 1950s, they, too, had moved to the mainland, their stations deactivated.

It is the nature of islands to change, especially islands as organic and tenuous as these sandy barriers. Islands change by the minute, pushed and pulled by tides, scattered by winds. The tide changes from ebb to flood approximately every six hours; it is a phenomenon of moon gravity, push and pull. But in addition to the daily tides, there are geological highs and lows, measured not by hours but by millennia, driven not by moon gravity but by the warming and cooling of the planet.

We are in a period of flood tide. Polar ice is melting and sea level is rising worldwide. The islands, over time, respond by moving westward. Just as we have high tides and low tides each day, there also are geological high and low tides, periods when sea level rises and then retreats. Geologists say that over the past 1.8 million years, sea level has risen and fallen six times. At the time of the last great low tide the sea level was 400 feet lower than it is today, and the Atlantic beaches were sixty miles east of where they are now, on the Continental Shelf.

Our rising geological tide has manifested itself over the past century and more, and it has come with unexpected consequences. In the case of the Virginia barrier islands, it has created a wilderness.

Chapter 1: The Landscape

The Atlantic at dawn, Assateague Island
22 March 2021
Photograph by the author

This is where the world ends. This is where the world begins.

I stepped out of the boat into the ocean current, the water cold and insistent, pushing me toward the inlet as I held the gunwale of the boat and steadied myself, checking my balance, my bare feet burrowing into the sand as the current sent loose grains seaward. I released the gunwale and stepped toward the beach, pausing to enjoy the power of the ebbing tide as it neared the inlet, constricted between the north end of Cedar Island and the south end of Metompkin, the great volume of water that earlier lay languid and slack in Longboat Channel and Burtons Bay, now moving with dispatch after building up behind the islands, flowing eastward toward this narrow opening between spits of sand, gaining velocity as moon gravity pulls, finally releasing itself as it stumbles over shallow bars. The water hisses and rolls, carrying sand, finally collapsing as it tumbles over itself and disappears beneath a blanket of white.

I must have been ten, and this is how I spent most of my summertime Saturdays. My father liked to fish for flounder, and I preferred to be on the beach, contemplating the ocean, speculating as to what may lie beyond the horizon. He would nudge our little skiff up to the shallows just inside the inlet, and I would wade ashore with a beach towel and a bottle of water. Sometimes I would bring a friend, and sometimes my father would spend time on the island, but mostly I came by myself. Usually, I had the place to myself, but now and then there would be a boat anchored at the surfs edge and someone would be walking the beach.

I have nothing against mountains, but I prefer sand to rocks, subtlety to stridency. Mountains are imposing and overstated, geology flexing its muscles. I prefer instead the fragments of mountains – quartz, garnet, magnetite – washed down from the highlands to the coast, mixed with the calcium fragments of seashells and deposited in a narrow ribbon at the edge of the sea.

That is the stuff these islands are made of – the remains of ancient mountains and the remains of shells, geological detritus that takes on a new life in this curious edge where the land meets the sea. The sand of these islands is organic, with a life of its own, forever changing like an amoeba, constantly altering itself in response to pressures from outside.

It is the edge that fascinates me. Stepping out of my father's boat, I knew I was entering something wild and undefinable, the cold persistence of the ocean, the crash and roar, the hiss of retreat. I was at the edge of the world, but I knew there was more. The land had its limits; it ended here, defined by the longest lick of low tide. But the ocean was rife with possibilities. The ocean was the avenue, the future, the world without end. I prefer to explore the ocean from its edge, and I prefer to explore land from its edge. I have no desire to go to sea, to experience a nautical version of crossing the great prairies. I prefer to be here where one world ends and another begins, to live in this rough edge where land and sea collide.

It is important to be alone here, and to have as few reminders as possible of the nearness of civilization – that is, no roads, parking lots, boardwalks, hotels, tourists. Then I can concentrate on the real issues: the ebb and flood, the promise of the horizon, the remarkable power and energy that come from no discernable source. Standing alone at

The Landscape

the edge of the sea we are close to something we cannot define or comprehend, beginning to get our feet wet.

Few places remain on the east coast where you can stand on the edge – balanced between fastland and ocean – and not be reminded of the nearness of civilization. The barrier islands of Virginia are one of the few remaining places where you can do that. These islands are now our coastal wilderness, a landscape of islands, inlets, shallow bays, and vast meadows of spartina grass stretching some one hundred miles from the north end of Assateague in Maryland south to the Virginia capes. The islands have their history, colorful and gaudy, but today they belong to the seabirds, to the myriad creatures of the tidal flats, and to those of us who find the need now and then to explore the edge and to look toward the horizon and speculate as to what might lay beyond.

Eighteen separate islands line the coast, ranging from Sinepuxent Bay at the northern tip of Assateague Island in Maryland to Smith and Fisherman Islands at the entrance to the Chesapeake Bay. The islands are buffers; they absorb the great energy of the Atlantic Ocean. The islands are low-slung and built to move, and when a storm ravages the ocean and sends it landward, the islands move with it, taking a punch. When the storm clears, the islands will still be there, but perhaps in a different configuration – an inlet closed, an inlet opened, a vast overwash fan created where, come spring, piping plovers, black skimmers, and terns will nest in the shell litter, their speckled eggs disappearing into the storm debris.

The islands are separated by inlets, narrow passageways maintained by the coming and going of the tide, scoured openings between islands that perhaps are deep enough to allow boats to navigate, but capricious enough to give mariners second thoughts about doing so. The inlets are busy places, a meeting ground where the sluggish waters of the inland bays comingle with the worldly currents of the ocean.

Behind the islands are shallow bays, tidal creeks, and great prairies of saltmarsh cordgrass, *Spartina alterniflora*, which make their own contribution to the buffering effect of the barrier island system. The marshes, like the islands, absorb energy, slow the flood waters, and have a calming effect when nature becomes obstreperous. They also are a great nursery, the bread basket of the coastal ecosystem. Grasses grow luxuriantly in spring and summer, thick masses of sun sponge, capturing energy stored in their green leaves and stems, and then, in winter, proceed to rot, and thus pass along all it had collected and earned to a new generation of saltmarsh life.

The spartina marshes are threaded by little waterways called drains, which is pronounced dreens, and it is the job of dreens to distribute the wealth of the benefactor spartinas to countless saltmarsh animals. The marsh is the nursery of the saltwater coast, producing the young of many commercially valuable fish, and also those of zero commercial value, but valuable just the same.

When the spartina is broken down by bacteria in winter it creates a planktonic soup called detritus, a cocktail of bacteria, epiphytic algae, and the cellulose particles of digested spartina, and this forms the broad base of the saltmarsh food chain, feeding everything from clams and oysters to fiddler crabs and menhaden. Oysters grow in clusters called rocks, often exposed at low tide. Clams burrow beneath the surface of the tidal flat and send up two siphons, one of which inhales energy-rich detritus, while the other expels waste. Menhaden are omnivores that swim in tight schools with their mouths open, filter feeding on phytoplankton (plant material) and zooplankton (animal material). All of these creatures are like the little robot vacuum cleaners they sell on TV. They suck in the good stuff and the bad stuff, thus making the saltmarsh a cleaner place.

In addition to the barrier islands, the seaside has numerous inner islands. The barriers in the southern part of the chain, roughly from Hog Island southward, tend to be farther from the mainland, so there are more inner islands as well as wide, shallow bays. Mockhorn is a large island with a ridge running north and south east of the village of Oyster. Farther north, Revels Island and Sandy Island lie between Parramore and the mainland. These bays, tidal flats, and marshes that separate the islands from the mainland are called the Broadwater.

The Landscape

The inner islands mainly have spartina grasses, but some have higher ridges that are home to salt meadow hay (*Spartina patens*) and shrubs such as saltwater bush, wax myrtle, and cedar. Some of the islands have forested communities called hummocks, or hammocks. Many of these are now called ghost forests because the pines that grew there years ago are dying, leaving pale gray apparitions as sentinels in the landscape. As sea level rises, lower marshes become tidal flats as the spartina dies. On higher land, *S. patens* gives way to *S. alterniflora*. The ghost forests will one day become spartina marshes, and land that is arable today will one day grow *S. patens*, tubular little plants called *Salicornia*, and succulents such as sea oxeye. And it's all a matter of inches in elevation. Elevation determines plant type. I remember many years ago walking the family farm with my father, and he gestured toward a field of salt meadow hay. "We grew sweet potatoes there when I was your age," he told me.

Chapter 2:
Past Presence

Quite a few years ago I was walking a farm field where my uncle grew corn and soybeans. It was early spring and my uncle had just turned the soil, and an overnight rain had scoured the field. It was the perfect time to look for artifacts.

Here on the Virginia coast we have a certain reverence for rocks, and the reason is that we have very few native stones. By the time rocks reach the coast they are ground down and weathered to sand, fragments of rocks, fragments of mountains. So, to find a rock is in many instances akin to finding an archaeological treasure. In the mountains, a rock in a farm field is an obstacle. On the coast, a rock in a farm field is a symbol of life.

It doesn't always work out that way. Sometimes a rock is a remnant of an old road bed, sometimes it is all that is left of the bulldozed foundation of a building, sometimes a rock traveled as ballast in a schooner. But now and then, on rare occasions, it can be an object created by the human hand. I saw an oval of quartz shining in the morning sun, glistening against the black earth. I nudged it with my boot and discovered that the oval was the tip of a much larger stone. I picked it up, wiped it off on my pants, and realized I was holding a perfectly shaped little axe head about four inches long and two inches wide. The blade was remarkably sharp, and although it was a fairly coarse rock, it had been worn smooth. The blunt end was flattened and hammer-like, and it tapered gracefully to a blade that was dark and polished from use.

I find it remarkable that some talented toolmaker had created this axe, had used it in his daily life one thousand or more years ago, and it had rested here for centuries, covered by sandy topsoil, until my uncle's plow exposed it and I happened to stumble upon it. This rock, this tool, was last touched by human hands before the arrival of Europeans and Africans, long before this field had been plowed for the first time, and now I'm standing here with the maker's axe in my hands, and I can feel the kinship.

I wonder what he used that axe for. It was not nearly substantial enough for clearing fields, but it could have been used for butchering a deer, or it could have been used for a building project. Such is the mystery of surface finds in farm fields. Arrow and spear points have their obvious uses, but now and then something turns up that certainly must be a tool, but its use is an enigma. I once found a stone in the shape of an equilateral triangle, about three inches on each side and one inch in thickness. It looked much too businesslike to be a natural river stone, so I handled it for a while and soon found a notch on the top edge where my index finger felt comfortable, and another indention on the left side where my thumb fit perfectly. The lower edge of the triangle had obviously been worn, so I was holding a scraper of some sort, something that might have been used on hides, or perhaps to crush small grains or the roots of plants that were used in cooking.

Most of the tools and artifacts I have found were on the seaside, near the saltmarshes and bays that separate the mainland Eastern Shore from the barrier islands. I've spoken with archaeologists, who have told me that Native Americans had a strong presence along both the seaside and bayside of the peninsula, but their presence on the barrier islands is a mystery.

Helen C. Rountree and Thomas E. Davidson, in their 1997 book *Eastern Shore Indians of Virginia and Maryland* said Indians preferred fresh water swamps, because that was where they found emergent plants with edible roots, such as arum. Rountree and Davidson describe the landscape in terms of "major ecological zones." The Indians favored dry land, marshes and swamps, and waterways. When the European colonists arrived, they sought waterways and dry land, especially waterways deep enough to float ships, and dry land in close proximity to the waterway. In other words, the settlers were seeking necks of land, the original American community. (See Chapter 17, Peninsulas in Repose – The Necks of the Eastern Shore.)

Shell middens on both the seaside and bayside provide ample evidence that the local natives depended heavily on shellfish in their diet, and they hunted and foraged in the swamps and marshes that separate the upland and the barrier beaches. Little is known about their presence on the islands themselves. They probably gathered bird eggs during the shorebird nesting season in spring, but there is little evidence to support that. For one thing, sea level has been rising for centuries, and the topography of the islands today is unlike it was four centuries ago, when contact with Europeans was first made. If the Native Americans maintained settlements on the islands during that period, they likely would be underwater today.

Archaeologists say that the presence of Native Americans in coastal Virginia dates back to at least 8000 B.C. Keith Egloff and Deborah Woodward, in *First People – The Early Indians of Virginia*, describe six different periods of early life: Early Archaic (8000 – 6000 B.C., Middle Archaic (6000 – 2500 B.C., Late Archaic (2500 – 1250 B.C.) and Early Woodland (1250 – 500 B.C.) Middle Woodland (500 – 900 A.D.) and Late Woodland (900 – 1600 A.D.).

Egloff and Woodward say coastal Virginia offered a unique environment, with a mix of upland, swamps and marshes, freshwater rivers, and saltwater creeks and bays. Native people gathered shellfish year around and caught fish during the warm months, drying them for future use. "By A.D. 1300 the Coastal Plain tribes had grown to form sedentary villages supported by small short-term hunting and gathering camps," they wrote. "Relying more and more on horticulture, they favored the floodplain and low-lying necklands of rich sandy soil for village sites."

Little remains of village sites today. Archaeologists have re-created residential patterns by locating posts that lie beneath the plowed layer of farm fields or other disturbed land. In doing so, they have discovered what building techniques might have been like when the Native People were progressing from a nomadic life to one of semi-permanent villages and farms.

Rountree and Davidson give this description of a pre-contact Native American dwelling:

> The preferred house shape was that of a loaf with rounded ends (oval floor plan and barrel roof); the two doors might be placed anywhere. Ordinary houses had one large room, in which "six to twenty" people slept at night; only chief's houses and temples had separate rooms in them, Saplings fifteen or so feet long were cut, debranched, and set in to holes several inches deep and a foot or so apart around the periphery of the intended building. Wooden crosspieces were then lashed on, parallel to the ground and a foot or so apart. The builders stood on the completed crosspieces to reach the higher levels, and eventually the weight of people working several feet up bent the sides and ends inward until they met. Either reed mats or strips of bark were lashed to the framework, overlapping so as to shed rain. A smoke hole was left in the center of the roof over the hearth, and low doors were left in the frame and its sheathing; both openings had their own moveable coverings.

Typically, natives would forage in the spring and early summer as berries and wild greens ripened, and then return to their towns or settlements where the women would plant garden crops and the men would clear fields for future planting. They used no soil additives, so the grounds were quickly depleted, at which time they would move to a new plot. They cleared only enough to allow sunlight to penetrate; crops would be planted around stumps and other obstacles.

The local people's first contact with Europeans probably came in the 1500s. If they happened to be standing on one of the barrier island beaches in 1524, they might have caught sight of Giovanni da Verrazano and his crew as they sailed north past the Virginia Capes without stopping. In 1546 an English ship was forced by a storm into the Chesapeake Bay and met thirty canoes with fifteen to twenty natives in each seeking friendly trade. In 1570-72 Spanish Jesuits sailed up the bay to establish a mission, and chances are good that they had contact with local fishermen. In the 1580s the English attempted to settle in coastal North Carolina, and the "lost colony" of 1587 could have migrated north to settle among the Chesapeakes. Jamestown was settled in 1607, and in 1608 Captain John Smith explored the Eastern Shore and documented the lives of the Accomacks and Occohannocks, the two principal tribes of the isolated Eastern Shore.

Rountree and Davidson write in depth about the early relationships between the native people and the white settlers, including legal and business dealings and government matters, but there were no wars between natives and whites on the Eastern Shore as there were elsewhere. As Rountree and Davidson put it, "Native American people were flooded out of their territory by a larger population of Europeans."

The Woodland Farm Study

In 1997 and 1998 Dennis Blanton of the William & Mary Center for Archaeological Research (WMCAR) headed a study at Thomas Wharf on Woodland Farm, which at the time was owned by The Nature Conservancy. Woodland Farm is on the seaside in Northampton County and is bordered by Upshur Creek on the south, Greens Creek on the north, and the Machipongo River on the east. Route 600 is the western boundary. Thomas Wharf is one of the few deep-water ports on the seaside and was a busy shipping point during the era of sail. Numerous surface finds over the years suggested an occupation by Native Americans back to the Middle Woodland period and forward to the historic contact era of post 1600.

Blanton's study was the first archaeological site formally recorded in Northampton County and now likely ranks as the most intensively studied prehistoric habitation across the Eastern Shore. "The results generated thus far establish the significance and richness of a deep Native American history in this region, yet it is a heritage that remains woefully understudied," he said in a report issued in 1999.

Not surprisingly, considering its location, the Woodland site provides ample evidence that the people living centuries ago depended heavily on a diet of fish and shellfish. "From the proliferation of shell in the associated sheet midden, one can infer that exploitation of nearby tidal wetlands was an important activity," Blanton wrote. "Indeed, it is not unrealistic to suggest that the vast wetlands adjacent to the site today were only beginning to develop by about 2000 BP."

According to Blanton, the most intensive occupation of the site took place in the Late Woodland period, from about A.D. 1000 to 1400. Remains found in pits indicate that people depended heavily on coastal resources, augmented by small game and plant food, although there was no evidence of cultigens, such as corn. "Continued reliance on natural foods as dietary staples is a pattern characteristic of Townsend occupations and one that reflects the bounty of coastal environments," wrote Blanton. "In effect, food crop production was delayed as an attractive option for Eastern Shore groups until very late in the prehistoric period."

Blanton believes that the settlement at Thomas Wharf is likely one of many to have been distributed throughout the area. "Even though occupation of the site in the late Woodland was somewhat intensive, Thomas Wharf would have been among several locations within the general vicinity where the occupants would have stopped over on their annual rounds to collect food," wrote Blanton. "It remains to be determined, but there is every likelihood that other related encampments are to be found on barrier islands and in interior settings."

There were a few surprises among the findings. Items such as glass trade beads dating from the late 16th to early 17th century as well as pipe stem fragments indicating ties to northern regions. In the case of the beads, they originated as far north as the sphere of Dutch trade in Pennsylvania and New York. "Establishing this link is one of the significant contributions of the Thomas Wharf work and one that stands to come as a revelation to many scholars," said Blanton. "Also, at this point, it can be surmised that Thomas Wharf was also the site of a small contact-period farmstead, an aspect of local history we know little about anywhere on the Eastern Shore."

The Mockhorn Island Clovis Site

In 2001, archaeologist Darrin Lowery discovered a complete crystal quartz Clovis projectile point on the western shoreline of Mockhorn Island. This leaf-shaped, fluted artifact is representative of a group of Paleoindians who are believed to have had an encampment 13,000 years ago at a site on what today is Mockhorn Island. It was an astounding find in that the general consensus is that any encampment that old on the Eastern Shore would have long been underwater.

In 2009 the Chesapeake Watershed Archaeological Research Foundation received a multiyear grant from the Threatened Sites Program of the Virginia Department of Historic Resources to conduct research on Mockhorn. The Smithsonian's National Museum of Natural History provided additional funding and other assistance. Between October 2010 and January 2013, researchers spent sixty-nine days on Mockhorn digging core samples on the shoreline of the island and on the mainland west of Magothy Bay. Also, twenty-one test units one meter square were set up in a transect parallel to the shoreline near where other Clovis artifacts had been found, and at low tide, sediment was wash-screened using quarter-inch mesh.

The research produced a wide assortment of tools including projectile points, scrapers, knives, cobbles, wedges, drill bits, and other Paleoindian artifacts. The remarkable thing about the find, other than its age, is that there is evidence that the Clovis people were involved in boat building and/or boat repair. The stone tools found by the researchers were commonly used in woodworking, suggesting that the Clovis people were building canoes, rather than burning out logs as is commonly assumed. Researchers further found evidence through pollen analysis that 13,000 years ago birch trees grew in the area, supporting the idea that Paleoindians on what is now Mockhorn Island could have been making birchbark canoes.

A number of the tools found on Mockhorn show signs of being heated, and possibly were used to apply melted birch pitch or tar on boats to seal them. Birch pitch is the oldest known human-produced adhesive, according to a report on the project. The report was included in a book published by the University of Utah Press in 2017 titled *In the Eastern Fluted Point Tradition*, edited by Joseph A.M. Gingerich.

Birchbark canoes are widely thought of as a creation of the Maine woods. Could they have been made 13,000 years ago on the Virginia coast? Such are the mysteries of history and science. Much of history involves following a paper trail – court records, wills, census data, written narratives – and there obviously is no paper trail leading to the lives of Clovis people.

Investigating this aspect of history is akin to space exploration. The paper trail has taken us only so far, perhaps an orbit of the planet Earth. But there is much farther to go, much more to explore and to learn. And this time the trail will be explored through science, or rather a coupling of science with equal parts intuition and imagination. And on Virginia's Eastern Shore, one feels that this journey is just beginning.

Chapter 3: Assateague & Chincoteague Islands

Chincoteague and Assateague have a symbiotic relationship. Chincoteague is a thriving, growing resort town drawing hundreds of thousands of visitors a year. Assateague is the reason for Chincoteague's good fortune.

Here we have another example of how changes in transportation bring about changes in society. Prior to 1962 Chincoteague was for the most part a fishing community, known nationally for its delicious, salty Chincoteague oysters. Assateague, which once had a small village of its own, had been purchased by the federal government in 1943 and became part of America's National Wildlife Refuge System. Dikes were built, impoundments were created, and ducks and geese came in great numbers each fall.

Then, in 1962, an abandoned steel bridge near Atlantic City, New Jersey, was purchased by a group of local officials and businessmen, and it was moved section by section to Chincoteague and used to span the channel between Piney Island and Assateague. A road was built on Assateague leading to the beach, and Chincoteague was forever changed. In 1965 President Lyndon B. Johnson signed legislation creating Assateague Island National Seashore, and Chincoteague's economy began its inevitable shift toward tourism. By 1985 two million people a year were travelling down Maddox Boulevard, crossing Piney Island, and taking the bridge over the channel to Assateague. In summer they came for the beach, in fall and winter they came for birds. In all seasons they came to see the famous Chincoteague ponies.

Today Chincoteague is a pleasant blend of seafood harvesting and tourism. Oysters are still grown in the shallow bays and coves, but more often than not in controlled aquaculture settings. They still have that sweet salty flavor that conveys a hint of the saltmarsh. Tourism, though, is what drives the economy, not only for the town but for adjacent communities on the Eastern Shore. Visitors to Chincoteague do not always stay on the island, but now and then venture north and south, perhaps to have lunch in Pocomoke City or Onancock.

Chincoteague has a few national chain hotels today, but it still has a small-town ambiance, a place where families are welcome. Many of the older hotels are still in business, providing something of a throwback feeling, offering modern comforts within a context of the last century.

Hotels are like cars. As they age, most simply get old and wear out, but a few turn out to be classics, capturing something of an earlier time and making it relevant today. The Refuge Inn is like that. It was built in 1973 by the Leonard family, whose ancestors founded the Leonard Fish Company, one of the pioneering seafood dealers on the island. Today, the inn is being operated by the third generation of Leonards, who are very active in the community. The inn is a welcoming, comfortable place, and the old metal room keys recall the 1970s in a way that is reassuring. I would much prefer to unlock my door with a stout hunk of metal rather than by waving a piece of plastic at it. When the Leonards decide to re-decorate a room, you know the wallpaper pattern will be determined by a family discussion in the living room, not by executives in the corporate office in Chicago.

Assateague and Chincoteague have had a long relationship. Assateague is the barrier island, beginning on the south at Tom's Hook and running north some thirty-five miles into Maryland, ending at the Ocean City Inlet. Chincoteague is an inner island today, but before Tom's Hook began migrating south in the late 1800s, the south end of Chincoteague fronted the ocean. Chincoteague is much smaller, but early settlers found the soil there more fertile than on sandy Assateague. Native Americans used both islands for fishing and hunting, but probably did not live on the islands, even though the local tribe was called the Chincoteagues, or Gingoteeks.

Historian Kirk Mariner, in his 1996 book *Once Upon an Island*, explained that the islands were too small to accommodate the Indians' way of life. "The Indians of the peninsula did not live in permanently settled villages, but migrated among several places as game and fields demanded," he wrote. "After a couple of years of planting one field, they would move to another, taking with them the wooden framework of their 'houses' and the mats they used to cover those frames...neither Chincoteague nor Assateague had enough area to provide the range they needed for hunting or the kind of soil needed for their crops. Even so, both Chincoteague and Assateague were undoubtedly important to the Indians, known to them and used by them."

Mariner believed that much of what is now the northern part of Accomack County on the seaside was referred to as Chincoteague, which means "large stream" or "inlet." Assateague means "a place across." A Baptist church founded in 1786 near the mainland community of New Church was named Chincoteague Baptist Church.

The first English settler to own land on Chincoteague was Thomas Welburn, a prominent landowner who lived on the mainland across Chincoteague Bay. In colonial days, the process of becoming a landowner involved obtaining a patent from the authorities of the colony, and then building a home and garden on the tract. The house had to be at least twelve feet square, and the garden had to be one acre of fenced land. The house had to be lived in for at least a year.

Thomas Welburn obtained a patent for Chincoteague Island from his father-in-law, Daniel Jenifer, and on January 20, 1680 took a small crew of workers to the western shore of Chincoteague and began clearing land and building a house. According to Mariner, the first white man to live on Chincoteague was Robert Scott, whom Welburn installed as his tenant. Scott apparently lived in the house for the requisite year, and then moved out. Mariner wrote that Edward Hammond, a fisherman from Maryland, visited the site in the fall of 1681, spent the night in the abandoned building, and found that Native Americans had been using the house and enjoying the corn that Welburn had planted.

Welburn's patent was later rescinded, and in 1691 the island was deeded to William Kendall and Major John Robins of Northampton, each taking one-half of the island. Kendall received the northern half, Robins the southern portion. Mariner wrote that all three of the men – Welburn, Kendall, and Robins – who vied for the island were wealthy individuals who owned large tracts of land, owned slaves, and lived in lavish homes. Why did they want a remote marshy island that was difficult to reach? Because Chincoteague Island would provide excellent pasture for their livestock.

"Virtually every island of the Shore was acquired for this purpose," wrote Mariner. "By the end of the (17th) century, hogs, sheep, and horses were roaming most of the island marshes of the peninsula."

The Pony Roundup

The Chincoteague Volunteer Fire Company was chartered in 1925 after two fires greatly damaged the downtown area. The company was authorized by the town council to hold a carnival to raise money to buy equipment, and it was decided to hold the carnival at the time of the annual pony roundup, when ponies that roamed the marsh islands would be rounded up and sold. The ponies were privately owned, but the roundup attracted a crowd, and the company hoped to eventually have a herd of its own to sell.

The first pony penning sponsored by the firemen was held on July 30, 1925. It was a huge success and thus began the modern era of the roundup, the pony swim, and the sale, which attracts thousands of people to the islands and serves as the major fundraiser for the fire company.

While the modern era of pony penning began with its association with the firemen in 1925, pony penning was an ancient tradition on the islands. Ponies, as well as cattle, sheep, goats, and hogs, were pastured on the barrier islands, where fences were not needed. The animals would be rounded up each spring or summer, branded, gelded, sheared (in the case of sheep), and generally given a physical checkup.

If the modern era of pony penning began in 1925, when did the ancient era begin, and what did the two eras have in common? It is likely that the roundups began shortly after the island was granted. Robins and Kendall received title to the land in 1691. If they moved expeditiously to pasture livestock there, the first pony penning could date to the late 1600s. If not, then certainly to the early 1700s.

The ancient era pony roundups were part of the business of keeping livestock as a money-making enterprise. It was necessary, at least once a year, to round up the animals – conduct a census, in effect – and cull the herd, selling some and branding the new additions. Over the years – again, no one knows when – pony penning became an occasion to have a celebration, a great gathering. What we do know is that by 1835, pony penning had been going on for so long at least one writer termed it an "ancient" custom.

In July 1835 Thompson Holmes wrote an article for the journal *Farmers' Register* titled "Some Account of the Wild Horses of the Sea Islands of Virginia and Maryland". It is the earliest known news media account of pony penning. Holmes was a native of Northampton County and a doctor. He was born in 1780 and in 1805 married Elizabeth A. Stockley of Accomack and was appointed doctor attending that county's almshouse. He was named a county justice of the peace in 1807 and served as county sheriff from 1828 to 1830. In 1811 he bought a farm called *Pharsalia* on Chincoteague Bay near what is now the community of Captain's Cove. He also owned grazing land on the north end of Chincoteague Island. Holmes Presbyterian Church in Bayview was named in his honor in 1846.

Farmers' Register was a periodical dealing with agricultural issues published roughly from 1832 to 1842 by Edmund Ruffin, a pioneering soil scientist. Ruffin was a wealthy landowner in Prince George County, Virginia, a slave owner and ardent secessionist who claimed to have fired the first shot of the Civil War at Ft. Sumpter in April 1861.

Holmes had lived at *Pharsalia* for twenty-four years and was preparing to move his family to Pennsylvania when he was asked by Ruffin to write an article on pony penning. Holmes had attended pony pennings on Assateague and owned Chincoteague ponies and he agreed to write about the event and the customs that were part of it. Holmes submitted a florid narrative in keeping with the style of the era:

> The horses have been gradually diminishing in number, by neglect, until on one island, they are nearly extinct; and the rustic splendor, the crowds, and wild festivity of the Assateague horse-pennings, scarcely retain a shadow of their ancient glory. The multitudes of both sexes that formerly attended those occasion of festal mirth, were astonishing. The adjoining islands were literally emptied of their simple and frolic-loving inhabitants, and the peninsula itself contributed to swell the crowd, for fifty miles above and below the point of meeting. All the beauty and fashion of a certain order of the female population, who had funds, or favorites to command a passage, were sure to be there. All who loved wild adventure -- whose hearts danced at the prospect of a distant water excursion, and a scene of no ordinary revel, where the ocean rolled his billows almost to their feet; all who had a new gown to show, or a pretty face to exhibit, who could dance well, or sing; belles that sighed for beaux, and beaux that wanted sweethearts; all who loved to kiss, or to be kissed, to caress, or be caressed; all, in short, whose hearts delighted in romance, without knowing its name, hurried away to this anxiously expected scene of extravagant jollity, on the narrow thread of beach that the ocean seemed, every moment, threatening to usurp. You can scarcely imagine, sir, the extravagant enthusiasm with which this exciting sport was anticipated and enjoyed. It was a frantic carnival, without its debauchery. The young of both sexes, had their imaginations inflamed by the poetical narratives of their mothers and maiden aunts, who in their more juvenile days were wont to grace those sylvan fetes, of the mad flight of wild horses careering away along a narrow, naked, level sand-beach at the top of their speed, with manes and tails waving in the wind before a company of mounted men, upon the fleetest steeds, shouting and hallowing in the wildest notes of triumph, and forcing the affrighted animals into the angular pen of pine logs, prepared to enclose them: and then the deafening peals of loud hurras from the thousand half-frenzied spectators, crowding into a solid

mass around the enclosure, to behold the beautiful wild horse, in all his native vigor subdued by man, panting in the toils, and furious with heat, rage and fright; or hear the clamorous triumphs of the adventurous riders, each of whom had performed more than one miracle of equestrian skill on that day of glorious daring -- and the less discordant neighing of colts that had lost their mothers, and mothers that had lost their colts in the *melee* of the sweeping drive, with the maddened snorts and whinnying of the whole gang -- all, all together, formed a scene of unrivalled noise, uproar and excitement, which few can imagine who had not witnessed it, and none can adequately describe.

Pony penning in those days was held on Assateague, not Chincoteague, and the famous pony swim was still far into the future. Like today, the ponies were sold, but the proceeds did not benefit the local fire company but rather the person who owned the animal. Sheep pennings were also held on Assateague and neighboring Wallops, and on some of the southern islands as well. After being rounded up and penned, the sheep would be sheared and the wool sold to local buyers.

The ponies that sold were taken by barge to the mainland, and rather than being pets, many were used for work or transportation. Holmes said the small ponies of Assateague made good work animals because they could perform equal labor as larger horses, but required less feed. Here he gives a description of the Assateague pony circa 1800:

> They are hardy, rarely affected with the diseases to which the horse is subject, perform a great deal of labor, if proportioned to their strength, require much less grain than common horses, live long, and are, many of them, delightful for the saddle. I have a beautiful island pony, who for fifteen years has been my riding nag in the neighborhood and upon the farm, who has given to my daughters their first lessons in equestrian exercise, and has carried us all many thousands of miles in pleasure and safety, without having once tripped or stumbled; and he is now as elastic in his gait, and juvenile in his appearance, as he was the first day I backed him, and is fatter than any horse I own, though his labor is equal, with less than two-thirds of their grain consumption, and to one unskilled in the indications of a horse's teeth, he would pass readily for six or seven years old.

My regrets at parting with this noble little animal, are those of the friend.

A third Eastern Shore community shared a relationship with Chincoteague and Assateague. Franklin City was built on a point of marsh north of the community of Greenbackville, and this was the islands' conduit with the wider world. Seafood was shipped to Franklin City, and when the railroad opened in 1876 it ushered in Chincoteague's original era of tourism.

Franklin City was named for Judge John Franklin, who owned the land where the community was built. Franklin gave half of his land to the Worcester Rail Road as an enticement to extend the rail from Snow Hill to the shores of Chincoteague Bay. The railroad opened on April 7, 1876, making it the first time a community on the Eastern Shore of Virginia could be reached by rail. Eight years later the NYP&N extended its line down the spine of the peninsula, linking by rail barge with points south.

The railroad terminated at a pier just five miles by boat from Chincoteague, and Franklin City quickly became a shipping point for seafood and other goods. The steamer *Widgeon* was put into service, ferrying not just merchandise between the island and the mainland, but passengers as well. It was no coincidence that the famous Atlantic Hotel opened on Chincoteague within a few months of the coming of the railroad, and by the 1890s the *Widgeon* was averaging more than 4,000 passengers a year.

The railroad also had a more unusual cargo. During pony penning, ponies that were sold to buyers on the mainland were taken by barge to Franklin City and were delivered to their new owners by rail. The *Peninsula Enterprise* gave this account in a February 1926 article on Chincoteague ponies:

> In August of each year, a pony penning takes place. All the ponies from the island are rounded up. The unbranded colts are then branded with the initial of the owner by the use of a hot branding iron. This day has been highly advertised and draws a large crowd of sightseers and those interested in the sale and

purchase of the Chincoteague ponies. Buyers are present from as far north as Canada and as far south as Florida. The number present at a pony penning ranges from one thousand to three thousand persons. From one hundred to two hundred ponies are sold to the various buyers. The price paid ranges from fifty to a hundred and fifty dollars, depending upon the age, weight and condition of the pony. Crates are constructed on barges and the sold ponies are driven aboard and are pulled by tugboats across the bay to Franklin City, Va. Here the ponies are placed in cars and shipped to their destination. For speed, endurance, longevity of life and beauty in form and color, the Chincoteague pony is beyond compare.

The modern era for Chincoteague began in the 1920s. In November 1922 the toll road linking the island with the mainland opened, with Governor E. Lee Trinkle coming to cut the ribbon. Two destructive fires damaged many buildings in the downtown area, but these were soon replaced with new, modern structures. The Chincoteague Volunteer Fire Company was formed in 1925, and that summer marked the beginning of the modern pony roundup, the swim, and the auction. It is a tradition that dates back to the colonial era, but it still today is a reason for people to gather and to celebrate.

The Assateague Village

Prior to the creation of the wildlife refuge and national seashore, Assateague had a small residential community for more than two centuries. About twenty-five families lived in a village scattered around the lighthouse. Some of the residents worked for the government, either at the lighthouse or the life-saving station, and later the coast guard station. Some worked at a guano factory at Tom's Hook, but most worked on the water, harvesting oysters in Tom's Cove. The villagers kept vegetable gardens and took advantage of the abundant game and fish literally in their own back yard.

There were two stores, a church, and beginning in 1890, a school. Dr. John W. Field moved to the island in 1893 and built a home there. He taught grades one through six in a one-room schoolhouse, and his impact on the island, and that of his family, had a profound effect on the community.

Field began acquiring property on the island around 1891 and by the time he died in 1912 his family owned nearly all of the Virginia portion of Assateague Island. In *Once Upon an Island* Kirk Mariner writes that when originally patented in 1687, the Virginia part of Assateague contained approximately 3,500 acres. When it was sold to the government in 1943 in contained 8,808 acres. The difference, according to Mariner, was a result of two factors. First, many older parcels of land were broken down into smaller components over the years and were abandoned and reverted to the state. Second, Assateague had grown substantially over the centuries, making new land available.

"The new acres, like the old reverted lands, could be obtained by "warrant" from the state, and most of what the Fields purchased came not from individuals but from the Commonwealth of Virginia," wrote Mariner.

John Field, the physician, who began the family's Assateague acquisitions around 1891, was highly respected in the community. His son, Samuel H. Field, who inherited the holdings, was not. Sam Field lived and worked in Baltimore, but he turned Assateague into a western style cattle ranch. Field claimed title to land down to the low water mark, put up "no trespassing" signs, and would not allow villagers to enter his property. This meant the villagers were cut off from oyster-rich Tom's Cove and the fish factories where many worked.

"Cut off from their main source of income, the villagers had little choice but to abandon their island, and by the end of 1922 the move to Chincoteague was complete," wrote Mariner.

Many of the homes were loaded onto barges and moved across the channel to Chincoteague, as was the Baptist Church, which was only three years old.

Sam Field hired Charles Oliphant, reportedly a cowboy from Wyoming, to be the overseer of his ranch, and his duties included enforcing the "no trespassing" policy. An article in the September 28, 1929 issue of the *Peninsula Enterprise* described him this way:

"Mr. Oliphant may be seen at any hour during the day or at night riding on a beautiful saddle horse. He dresses after the fashion of the Western cowboy and is withal a picturesque character, a man who knows his business and hard to replace. Two faithful collie dogs help him to round up the cattle or ponies when it is time to dip them in the cement tanks to rid them of ticks or to drive the calves into the corral before shipping."

The *Enterprise* reported that 200 two-year-old mules had been introduced to the island, along with 100 head of cattle. The mules and cattle were deemed unsatisfactory, however, because they required grain during winter. Native cattle and ponies were accustomed to grazing on marsh grass year around, and did not need supplemental food.

"A strange fact is that the wild cattle and ponies do not know how to eat, that is they have never seen corn or any other grain," wrote Marinus James. "They are used to marsh grass and get fat on that. Other feed is alien to their taste."

Sam Field's "no trespassing" policy extended to the owners of ponies being pastured on Assateague, and this created a major change in the pony penning ritual. Mariner wrote that the last roundup on Assateague took place on July 28, 1920. "Thus came to an end a tradition dating back two centuries or more," wrote Mariner. Mariner said the 1921 event did not take place, and by 1923 the owners of the ponies had been able to get them to Chincoteague for the first penning there.

It is not known how long Sam Field's cattle ranch existed, but the Field family once again had a profound effect on the island in 1943. By then the unpopular Sam Field had passed away, and his sister and heir, Nellie Field Burwell, sold more than 8,000 acres on Assateague, virtually the entire Virginia portion, to the federal government for $75,000, which had been raised through the sale of Federal Duck Stamps. And thus began Chincoteague National Wildlife Refuge, and the opening of a new era for Assateague.

The Oyster King

Tom Downing's mother and father were owned by Captain John Downing of Chincoteague Island, who had given them his surname. Fortunately for Tom, Captain Downing got religion and became convinced that it was impossible to be a good Methodist and an owner of slaves, so he not only gave Tom's parents their freedom, he also gave them a job building and maintaining a meeting house in upper Accomack County.

So, Tom, who was born in 1791, grew up a free young man on Chincoteague and set about making a living the same way most of the other free young men did on the island. He fished and signed clams and raked oysters. When he was young his parents sent him to a tutor, reportedly the same one Henry A. Wise went to a few years later. Wise, of course, would become the governor of Virginia.

It turns out that Tom was an outstanding waterman, coached, perhaps, by the man who had once owned his mother and father. Tom was successful at catching seafood, but his real interest was in what happened to the seafood after it was caught. He was especially fond of oysters, and when he wasn't working the oyster rocks of Chincoteague Bay, he was in the kitchen perfecting oyster stew.

Tom served in the army during the War of 1812, and when the war ended, he followed the army to Philadelphia, where he met his future wife, Rebecca West. Soon the couple moved to New York and rented an apartment at 33 Pell Street. Tom bought a small skiff and some oyster tongs, and each morning he would cross the Hudson to the oyster rocks in New Jersey, tong for oysters, and return with a load to sell to his regular customers before dark.

Tom had a reputation for excellent oysters, and his customer base grew quickly. In 1825 he opened an oyster cellar at 5 Broad Street in New York's financial district. Oyster cellars at the time had a reputation for being seedy places often frequented by prostitutes, but Tom's oyster house was scrupulously clean, nicely decorated, and welcoming to couples. It quickly became the place to go among the city's financial and political leaders. "Downing's was a place where oysters were eaten and deals were made," wrote Mark Kurlansky in his 2006 book *The Big Oyster – History on the Half Shell.*

Downing's Oyster House expanded in 1835, adding the two neighboring units at numbers 3 and 7 Broad Street. Downing's also began a catering business, which became very much in demand, building upon the popularity of the oyster cellar. When the celebrated English novelist Charles Dickens visited the city in 1843, Downing's was called.

"The city turned to Downing's, the most celebrated oyster cellar, to cater Dickens's introduction to twenty-five-hundred of New York's elite," wrote Kurlansky. "Downing's at that time was the caterer of official events. When a company opened, a ship was launched, a steam-powered vessel crossed the Atlantic, the Erie Railroad was extended north of the city...Downing's catered."

Thomas Downing, who grew up on Chincoteague Island raking oysters in Chincoteague Bay, had become one of New York's most successful businessmen. He died in New York City in 1866 at age 75, and The *New York Times* ran an extensive obituary, saying that his "eating house at Broad Street became known for the excellent viands to be procured there."

One thing the *Times* obituary did not mention was Downing's link with the Underground Railroad. Clint Smith, in his book *How the Word is Passed*, writes that Downing used his restaurant to provide cover for slaves heading north for freedom in Canada. He quotes a tour guide: "While he's upstairs dining and schmoozing, underneath his feet, his son George is hiding people in their cupboards."

And this presents an intriguing question. Thomas Downing had links to the Eastern Shore and New York. Harriet Tubman had links to the Eastern Shore and New York. Could the slaves Tubman was sending north possibly have been hiding in Downing's cupboards?

Chapter 4: Wallops Island

Few of Virginia's islands are widely known beyond the boundaries of the Eastern Shore. Exceptions would be Chincoteague and Assateague, famous for the ocean beach and wild ponies, and a third would be Wallops Island, because of its pioneering role in America's space program. During the early days of European settlement, the three islands were very much alike. There were a few dune lines forested with pine and cedar, and Assateague and Wallops and the south end of Chincoteague had their barrier beaches, but mostly there were great meadows of spartina grasses, salt water wetlands that ran from horizon to horizon. Like the other two islands, Wallops began its role under European stewardship as pastureland.

While Assateague is famous today for the wild pony roundup each July, in the early 18th century Wallops was known for its sheep roundup. Sheep roamed freely on the island, and in spring or early summer they would be rounded up, corralled, and sheared. Young animals would be branded, excess sheep would be sold for mutton, and the wool gained from the shearing process would be sold. Like pony penning, sheep penning was a reason for people to gather and celebrate. Hundreds of people would come from the mainland to help with the roundup, to meet friends, and to enjoy a great feast.

Wallops is the only barrier island to retain the name of the original patent holder. That would be John Wallop, who in 1672 received a patent for 1,450 acres on what was then known as Kekotank Island, or Accocomson Island. According to Ralph T. Whitelaw's *Virginia's Eastern Shore*, Wallop received subsequent patents in 1682 and 1692, which included all of the island and the adjacent marshes. Wallop left the island to his son, Skinner, and daughter, Sarah, and over the years parts of it were owned by the Kendall, Finney, and Watt families.

Whitelaw wrote that in 1889 the island was sold in its entirety to Wesley K. Woodbury of Wrightsville, Pennsylvania, and for many years after that the title was held by the trustees of the Wallops Island Association. The Pennsylvania group built a two-storied frame clubhouse on the island, along with a large pier, stables, and quarters for staff and caretakers. The Wallops Island Club took its place among the many private hunting and fishing clubs on the Eastern Shore seaside owned by northern interests. Whitelaw wrote: "As with many other of the island gunning and fishing clubs, a record of its activities and the incidents occurring there, through the years, would make most interesting reading if someone would make the effort to write it."

Most of the gunning clubs on the islands had memberships that centered around a common bond. The Broadwater Club on Hog Island consisted of Pennsylvania Railroad executives. The Accomac Club on Parramore was made up of thirty or so New York businessmen, many of whom were principals in the Fulton Street Fishmongers Association. The common bond of the Wallops Island Club seems to have been geographical; most of the members were from Pennsylvania.

The Wallops Island Association members purchased the island, which measured about one mile wide and seven miles long, for $8,000 in 1889. In the summer of 1890, they contracted with Chincoteague builder William Conant to build a two-storied clubhouse. On May 16, 1891 Conant presented them the keys to a handsome new clubhouse, and thus began the first summer season of the Wallops Island Club.

Unlike many of the other clubs, Wallops did not focus on waterfowl hunting, and it operated mainly during the spring and summer months. Visitors frequently included family groups, and the children were welcome. Local newspapers would make note of the opening of the club each spring.

A remarkable collection of photographs taken by Robert Stout of Bethlehem, Pennsylvania, in the first decade of the twentieth century, depict what life was like at the Wallops Island Club. Women and children were very much a part of the daily activities, which consisted of beach bathing, fishing, sailing, and having toy sailboat races. Robert Stout was obviously a skilled photographer, and he captured his subjects in a manner that was casual and without pretense. The subjects enjoyed the company of each other, and they enjoyed the landscape they were a part of.

Mr. Stout's family donated the collection of negatives to NASA, which made prints for the Eastern Shore Historical Society and for the Eastern Shore Barrier Islands Center in Machipongo, where the photographs are on display.

The Wallops Island Club was organized and managed by an association of businessmen, so it's not surprising that the club was governed like any good corporation. The shareholders held annual meetings, voted on business matters, approved budgets, and elected officers. The association was formed when the island was purchased in 1889 and it operated for nearly 60 years. Records of the annual meetings and the statements of assets and liabilities still exist, providing a vivid picture of the business side of running a barrier island club.

The annual meeting of the association in 1928 was held on October 1 at the Bellevue-Stratford Hotel in Philadelphia. At that time the club had a net worth of $77,907.63. Assets included 3,000 acres of land at $15 an acre, a clubhouse valued at $25,000, and other improvements including a stable and ice house, servant quarters and garage, boathouses, pumps, and docks. Floating assets included three launches, and livestock numbered 200 sheep at $4 and 100 ponies at $20. The only liabilities were several on-demand notes from banks.

The association employed local people for tasks that varied from housekeeping to tending the sheep and ponies. The manager for many years was the celebrated character from Chincoteague, Captain Benjamin Franklin Scott. Ben Scott was born on Hog Island in 1838 and worked as a farmhand and sailor before moving to Chincoteague with his wife Leah in 1860. He served in the Loyal Eastern Virginia Volunteers in the Civil War, and served his entire military duty on the Eastern Shore of Virginia, including at Cobbs Island, Onancock, and Chincoteague. After the war he returned to Chincoteague and became an oysterman. He and Leah had five children before she died at the age of 33 in 1880. He then married Leah's younger sister, Mary Jane, and their marriage produced four more children.

Ben Scott knew the Wallops Island area well, and there is evidence he had a cottage on the island prior to its sale to the association. In 1895 he accepted the position of manager, where he oversaw operation of the dining room, the small fleet of launches, and the staff of employees. He served as manager for twelve years before turning the job over to his son, Bud Scott. Ben moved back to Chincoteague where, at age 68, he began another career as a dairyman, delivering milk to the residents of Chincoteague in a horse-drawn wagon. Ben celebrated his 100th birthday in 1938 by leading the Firemen's Parade in Onancock. He died on January 17, 1944 at age 105, and at the time of his death was the island's most celebrated resident.

World War II brought changes to upper Accomack County, and these changes would eventually extend to Wallops Island. In 1942 the Navy began acquiring land on the mainland opposite Chincoteague to use as an auxiliary air station. By March 1943 the holdings covered more than 500 acres at the northern end of the causeway, and the Chincoteague Naval Auxiliary Air Station was officially commissioned. The station's mission was to provide support and training for carrier squadrons, but it also became a site for testing aviation ordnance and developments in gunnery. By the time the war ended more than 3,000 military and civilian personnel were working at the navy base. In 1957 the base officially became the Chincoteague Naval Air Station, and runways were extended to accommodate jet fighters.

Meanwhile, in May 1945, the National Advisory Committee for Aeronautics (NACA), which in 1958 became the National Aeronautics and Space Administration (NASA), leased 1,000 acres on the southern end of Wallops Island to use as a rocket proving ground. On the

Fourth of July in 1945 the first rocket was fired from Wallops beach over the Atlantic, and Wallops Island officially became a player in what would become America's space program. In 1949 NACA took possession of the entire island.

The Wallops facility consists of two components. Rockets are launched from the island, and the business and engineering operations are handled at what once was the navy base. NASA had planned to build a support facility at Assawoman to be closer to the launch site, but in 1959 the navy decided to close the base, so NASA took over the existing facility.

Since that July Fourth launch in 1945, close to 20,000 rockets have been launched from Wallops. In the past few years Wallops has expanded its mission, sending un-manned vehicles to study the atmosphere of the moon, and launching supply missions to the International Space Station. And with these newsworthy missions under its belt, the Wallops Flight Facility has assumed a higher profile. While Wallops once was known mainly for suborbital research, it now is enjoying life on a bigger stage.

"People began paying attention to Wallops in 2006 and 2007 when we did the first Minotaur launches from the Mid-Atlantic Regional Spaceport pad," says Keith Koehler, Wallops news chief. "But things really got going when Orbital Sciences Corp. was selected for the NASA Commercial Orbital Transportation Services (COTS) program and Commercial Resupply Services contract. In 2016 they tested the Antares rocket in April, and in September moved forward with the cargo supply mission to the International Space Station. In September we also launched the first interplanetary mission of the Lunar Atmosphere and Dust Environment Explorer (LADEE) aboard an Air Force Minotaur V rocket. It was a spectacular nighttime launch and it was watched by thousands of people along the mid-Atlantic coast."

The growth and success of the Wallops Flight Facility over the past few years raises an inevitable question. Will the next step for Wallops be human space flight? Keith Koehler chuckles at a question he has been asked many times, and he is carefully non-committal. "You never know. We would need to add a lot of infrastructure that we do not have now, and Kennedy Space Center already has this in place. It's not beyond the realm of possibility, but it would take a while to get there."

Chapter 5:
Cedar & Metompkin Islands

Most people who live on the Eastern Shore have a favorite waterfront escape. For folks along the bayside it could be Guard Shore west of Parksley, Weir Point on Onancock Creek, or Bayford, a favorite gathering place in Northampton. Often times, just a sandbar at low tide near the mouth of a creek would suffice.

On the seaside, people gathered many years ago at Red Hills, on Chincoteague Bay just south of the Maryland line. Chincoteague today is famous for the ocean beach on neighboring Assateague Island, but before the beach became a national seashore, Chincoteaguers crossed the bay and gathered at Red Hills. Usually, your favorite barrier island was the one closest and most accessible to where you lived. I grew up in Onley and our island of escape was Cedar, specifically the north end, just across the Inlet from Metompkin Island.

Over the years you become somewhat vested in your island domain. You learn where the most productive clam flats are, and you get to know the little creeks and guts that thread their way through the high marsh. You have drifted for flounder across all of the shallow bays, but you know now that if you begin at the red channel marker and drift toward green eleven on an incoming tide, you are likely to catch fish. You have walked the beach for hours, swam in the surf, and cast peeler crab baits to entice channel bass. The accumulation of all these things makes the place yours, like the granting of a patent from the authorities of the colony.

I learned the place names of all the creeks and guts of North Cedar when I was a child, and I still have them with me, a colorful accumulation of landmarks that didn't make it to the official maps and charts, but live on in memory. There was Punkin Gut, a shortcut to get from Folly Creek to Longboat Channel, but you had to time the tide just right. There was Teakle's Ditch, which was not really a ditch but just an opening that connected two small bays, cut long ago by an early settler named Teakle. There was Point of Rocks, which meant not stones but oysters. We had a duck blind on Knockknees Gut, which was wound so tight you could meet yourself coming the other way.

Cedar and Metompkin are east of the Accomac area, and these islands lack the maritime forests that mark the landscape of Parramore and Assateague. The islands are fluid, not solidly grounded, and they move with the storms and the seasons, as they are supposed to do. Each spring, after winter brings a few northeasters, you have to find your way around again. The furniture has been re-arranged.

Like all of the islands of Virginia's Eastern Shore, these two have had their affairs with humans. Both have had life-saving stations and coast guard stations. Cedar, on its south end, had a popular clubhouse where people gathered in the late 1800s. It later had a hotel called the Island House that operated as a satellite of the famous Hotel Wachapreague, a landmark built in 1902 that burned on July 1, 1978. Metompkin also had a hotel that operated for a few years in the late 1800s. Cedar Island had guano factories that supplied fertilizer made from oily menhaden fish to local farmers. Lots were sold on Cedar in the early 1950s and 1980s. Many of them are under water today.

Of the two islands, Cedar is the larger and has seen the most use by humans. In the 18th century it was noted for stands of large red cedars, which were used for rails and posts. By the mid-20th century the large trees were gone, replaced by thickets of small cedars, wax myrtle, and saltwater bush. When I was a child I played in the dunes on Cedar; I explored the dense, stunted cedar forest until the clouds of mosquitos drove me out. I camped out on Cedar during a northeaster when I was at home on leave from the air force in 1970. It still had dunes then because that's where I took shelter. The dunes are gone now, as is the forest, and the island has retreated westward as the sea has risen. But one day Cedar was envisioned as the next Cobbs Island, which was pounded into submission by storms in the 1890s. The *Richmond Times-Dispatch* published a story on August 25, 1907 titled "Cedar Island – The Place for the Tired and Weary.

> Out in the Atlantic Ocean, seven miles from the main land off the coast of Virginia, is a small pleasure resort, known as Cedar Island, which appeals to every one who, fond of sport and outdoor life, desires rest and recreation and surcease from business cares. Those who were wont to rusticate at Cobb's Island, a pleasant but vanishing memory, will find Cedar Island just such a place as Cobb's was before hungry waves devoured its sandy shores and put it out of commission. Out at Cedar Island one finds practically everything one cares to amuse one's self with in the summer; that is, to bathe, to fish, to sail and to rest on the broad beach always cooled by the sea breezes, and free for the most part from the invidious presence of the mosquito. The island is shaped something like a toboggan slide, seven miles long and 150 yards broad, which gives it the appearance of a huge yellow knife.

While Cobbs Island in its day attracted guests from all over the country, Cedar seems to have been popular with folks closer to home. Boats took local people on Sunday excursions to Cedar from Burtons Shore, Wachapreague, or the Folly Creek Landing. In August 1896 the *Peninsula Enterprise* was advertising evening trips to Cedar from Wachapreague. "The steam yacht *Gem*, commencing Monday, August 13th, will leave Wachapreague wharf every evening at 5 p. m., (until further notice) for Cedar Island, that favorite old resort, returning will leave the island at 10 p. m., giving more than five hours on the water and beach with ample opportunity for bathing, etc. Price for the round trip, 50 cents."

The Wachapreague Literary Club visited Cedar on June 13, 1891 for a dinner and program at the clubhouse. The *Peninsula Enterprise* reported that about forty members of the club, along with a number of guests, left Wachapreague at 10 a.m. and returned in the evening. One of the guests filed this report: "When supper was over at the Club house, and we had had our lovely sail back to Wachapreague, all declared, it one of the merriest days of life. We are now under the impression that every town and village ought to have a Literary Club or Society, and that they should all take a trip to the beach."

The Metompkin Hotel opened in 1894 and lasted for a few years, operated by several different people. An advertisement in the June 9, 1894 issue of the *Peninsula Enterprise* called it "a new ocean resort easy of access, by comfortable means and at moderate rates."

In January 1895 an item in the *Enterprise* said that the hotel was being put up for auction by the "mutual consent of the owners" in the February term of court in Accomac. The hotel was purchased by Robert L. Fletcher and Polk Lang. The latter was a well known businessman, sea captain, and general entrepreneur.

On July 20, 1895 the *Enterprise* reported that "The Metompkin Beach Hotel is now open. The best cooking is there. Good shooting and no finer surf bathing. Boat will leave Folly Creek to carry passengers every day at any hour. Proprietors Robert L. Fletcher and Polk Lang."

By the following summer the proprietors were "James Milliner and wife." And that sums up the brief lifespan of the Metompkin Beach Hotel. A hurricane in October 1897 destroyed the building, and in the words of a local newspaperman, "leveled (Cedar Island) to a mere flat breath of sand."

Fish Guano

The opening of the railroad in 1884 and the formation of the Eastern Shore of Virginia Produce Exchange in 1900 marked the beginning of a new era in agriculture. The railroad revolutionized transportation, and the Exchange made farmers think about marketing and producing crops of superior quality to get an edge over competitors.

The Eastern Shore's agricultural revolution was far reaching. It touched not only farmers and shippers and sales agents; it spawned an array of satellite industries. From 1900 through 1919 production of white potatoes in the two counties rose from 11,000 acres to 53,000 acres. Barrels were needed to get those potatoes to market, and most farming communities had at least one barrel factory.

To increase yields and grow a superior crop, farmers needed fertilizer, and much of it came from guano. Guano was made from the waste of birds and bats and was collected wherever there were nesting colonies. The gold standard of guano came from three tiny islands off the coast of Peru called the Chincha Islands, which were a nesting area for seabirds. The local waters were rich with fish and other sea life, and the birds would feed by day and roost at night on the islands, where there were no predators. Over many years, droppings accumulated to a depth of up to 200 feet.

Early in the 19th century farmers began using the Peruvian guano and chemists worldwide claimed that it was the finest fertilizer in the world. Unfortunately, the demand for Chincha guano was not sustainable. By the late 1870s the guano was gone and the seabird habitat had been ruined by the mining operation.

With the Peruvian supply exhausted, the fertilizer industry turned to islands in the Caribbean where colonies of seabirds nested. Crews, consisting mainly of black men, were being shipped out of coastal cities such as Baltimore and Norfolk to work on the guano islands. Shippers found that the guano trade was more profitable than hauling lumber, and the local men sent to dig the guano were paid $2 per day, not a bad wage back then.

In 1877 a Frenchman named Louis-Andre Angibaud developed a process for making guano from fish. Angibaud, working with a farmer and soil scientist named Alphonse Derome, used fish waste from canneries and wholesalers to make a fertilizer that was high in nutrients and much less expensive than bird guano, which had to be mined by hand and shipped great distances to be used.

Angibaud built a factory on the coast of France near La Rochelle, and soon was processing from twenty to forty tons of fish per day. The method involved grinding the fish to a paste, adding sulfuric acid, and then working in organic materials such as grape pulp. The mixture was stirred regularly and acted upon by bacteria, and in about four months reduced to a dry powdered fertilizer. The company that Angibaud founded is still in business today and is very popular among the wine growers of France.

It didn't take long for the news of Louis-Andre Angibaud's development of fish guano to reach the Eastern Shore, and guano factories were soon popping up on the seaside and the bayside. Within a few years, there were two guano factories on Cedar Island and others on Chincoteague, Assateague, and Tangier Island. Powell and Morse & Co, (later incorporated as the American Fish Guano Company) built a factory on the harbor at Huffman's Wharf (now Harborton), and had a fleet of ocean-going vessels ranging as far north as Maine. Most of the factories used menhaden, a small, oily fish common in the Chesapeake Bay and in the ocean.

Irish and sweet potatoes were driving the farm economy in those days, and fertilizer was in demand. As a contributor from Mappsville quipped in the March 1, 1884 edition of the *Peninsula Enterprise*, "Our farmers are making preparations to plant round potatoes on a more gigantic scale than was ever known before. We hear of nothing now almost but fertilizers, and nearly every other man is an agent."

Cedar Island was home to Fowler, Foote & Co., which was advertising dry ground fish guano in 1883 at $30 per ton. In 1887 Captain Orris A. Browne was offering Browne's Superior Cedar Island Guano at $40 per ton, delivered to a rail station near you.

Browne had his guano analyzed by a chemist with the Virginia Department of Agriculture and published the results in the January 9, 1884 issue of the *Peninsula Enterprise*. The result, said Browne, proved that the locally produced fertilizer was as good or better than the expensive Peruvian or Caribbean imports.

"By comparing the above (his analysis) with 146 different brands of fertilizers that have passed through the hands of the state chemist, none can compare in cheapness and quality with it," Browne claimed. It was, perhaps, an unfortunate choice of words regarding the hands of the state chemist, but Browne got his point across.

Browne not only manufactured guano on Cedar Island, he also raised cattle and sheep for many years. It was common practice to pasture livestock on the islands because the animals could live well on native plants, thus saving the costs of feed. But there also were drawbacks. The *Eastern Virginian*, a newspaper published in Onancock, reported in its October 26, 1878 issue that "one of the severest wind storms ever experienced in this section, and unquestionably the highest tide within the knowledge of any one now living" created severe flooding. "On Cedar Island nearly all the stock perished, Capt. O.A. Browne being a heavy loser. His loss there will be fully seventy-five cattle, and as many sheep." The newspaper reported that significant losses were expected on other islands as well.

The guano industry was especially suited for the barrier islands because the lengthy process of rendering dead fish into plant food had unpleasant consequences. It stunk. On the islands, as long as there was an offshore wind, the neighbors did not complain.

It is not known exactly where the guano factories stood on Cedar. The remains of the fish factory on Assateague can still be seen on the beach at Tom's Hook, far from the village that was near the lighthouse, but the remains of the Cedar Island factory are probably under water. We do know that a hotel and clubhouse were in operation on the south end in the 1880s. The guano factories were most likely on the north end.

Chapter 6:
The Revels Island Club

Revels Island, a marshy inner island near the south end of Parramore Island, was home to the Revels Island Club, which was incorporated in September 1884 as the Old Dominion Gunning and Angling Association. The name was changed in 1893.

The club owned a vast tract of marshland southwest of Parramore consisting of Revels Island and nearby Sandy Island, which lay south and west of Revels Island Bay. These inner islands are east of Upshur Neck, which extends north and south like a green finger of upland separating Machipongo River and Upshur Bay.

According to Ralph Whitelaw's history of the Eastern Shore, John Revell patented 450 acres on what at the time was called Home Island. Little is known about subsequent owners, but a story in October 1878 in the *Eastern Virginian* newspaper, published in Onancock, indicated that a violent storm created flooding on the seaside, and that livestock pastured on the island owned by Custis M. Dunton suffered heavy losses.

Dunton, in the November 19, 1883 issue of *Peninsula Enterprise*, listed the property for sale. He described the island as containing "700 acres of land well adapted to stock raising both winter and summer – 100 acres being upland – and improved by three comfortable dwelling houses." The asking price was $1,400.

In the August 1884 land transfers in Accomack County, Custis M.

Dunton sold 700 acres on Revels Island to Alexander R. Williams for $5,000, and 400 acres on Sandy Island for $100.

On September 27, 1884, Judge B.T. Gunter granted a certificate of incorporation to Williams and others, of Washington, D.C., under the name of the Old Dominion Gunning and Angling Association, and in October Williams transferred the property to the association. And thus began the Revels Island Club, one of the longest tenured gunning clubs on the seaside. It was in operation until the beginning of World War II.

Membership in the club was by purchase of stock, with each share assessed a certain amount each year to maintain and improve the property held in common, which consisted of a club house, boat house, docks, barns, pastures, and quarters for employees and guides. Unlike the more exclusive clubs such as the Accomac Club, membership was open to anyone who bought shares, and each May, in Pittsburgh, shares would be sold at public auction that had been forfeited because the annual assessment was in arrears. The Accomac Club had a membership of about thirty, and new members had to be voted in by existing members. The Revels Island Club had a membership of around 100, depending upon the annual rate of attrition.

A ridge of comparatively high land ran along the spine of Revels Island, roughly north and south, pretty much parallel to the beach on nearby Parramore. The club built its common areas along this ridge, and lots were sold to individuals who built cottages of their own. This area was just west of the south end of Parramore, tucked behind a sandy hook on the north edge of Quinby Inlet; a channel called The Swash separates Revels from the barrier beach.

There was a proposal at one time to build a road linking the island and the mainland. The *Peninsula Enterprise* of February 15, 1890 reported that a party of civil engineers was taken to the island "to determine the shortest and most practicable route for a road over the meadows from the island to the mainland." Apparently, the engineers determined that the road was not practicable, because there were no further stories about it.

When the NYP&N railroad opened in 1884, it made the seaside resorts of the Eastern Shore easily accessible. Visitors would board the train in New York or Wilmington in the morning and arrive in Keller that afternoon, where they would get transportation to Wachapreague to catch the launch to the islands. The Keller station served both the Revels Island Club and the Accomac Club, and the news media regularly recorded the arrivals and departures.

On May 18, 1897 Thomas G. Elliott filed this report for *Forest & Stream* magazine:

> Dr. J.C. French left for his home today, and reported never to have found better sport, especially on curlew. When about to leave he drew from his pocket two shells, remarking: "This is all I have left out of $20 worth. Don't you think it time I had gone?" The Doctor is a fine shot, and for the present it may be said that his love for the gun has been amply gratified.
>
> Arrivals for the week have been in part: Messrs. Edward Thompson and Edward Pigeon, with Mrs. Pigeon, of Long Island, members of the Revels Island Club, and Messrs. H.M. Spratley and G.W. Jacobas, members of the Accomac Club. Hon. W.K. Shiras returned today, reporting having a very pleasant trip and having fairly good shooting. It may be said of the members of the Revels Island and Accomac clubs, that their purpose in coming to our shore, for recreation and amusement is not a selfish one; but, on the contrary, it seems that they rather on every occasion strive to become useful by their liberality to our less fortunate citizens. It is said that the two clubs collectively represent millions upon millions of wealth. Such people are a blessing to any community they may enter.

Most of the members of the Revels Island Club were from Pennsylvania, and they include two men who came from very different backgrounds, but were well known American figures during the latter part of the nineteenth century.

George Shiras, III came from a prominent Pittsburgh family whose father was a Supreme Court justice. Shiras (who signed his name Shiras 3d) was himself a lawyer and politician, having served in the U.S. Congress, but he also enjoyed hunting, fishing, and was a keen naturalist. In Congress, he helped lay the foundation for legislation that later would become the Migratory Bird Law of 1916 and the Migratory Bird Treaty Act of 1918. He also was a nationally known wildlife photographer, and *National Geographic* magazine once devoted an entire issue to his work.

Hamilton Disston was the grandson of an English immigrant, whose father, Henry, was orphaned just days after arriving in the United States. Henry overcame much hardship to found Henry Disston & Sons, of Philadelphia, a major manufacturer of saw blades and files. Hamilton, who took over the business after his father's death, is best known for purchasing four million acres of land in south Florida with the intention of draining swamps around Lake Okeechobee and the Kissimmee, Caloosahatchee, and Miami rivers to convert the land to agricultural and residential use.

Shiras and Disston came from different backgrounds, but they had much in common. Both enjoyed hunting and fishing and they were drawn to the open spaces of the seaside Eastern Shore. Disston had a wide range of business investments, including real estate that was at or just below sea level, and steam powered pleasure craft. His steam yacht *Manatee* was frequently seen in the bays and creeks around Chincoteague and Wachapreague.

Both men were members of the Republican Party. Shiras was elected to the Pennsylvania state legislature in 1889, and then lost the Republican nomination for Congress in 1890. He later ran successfully and served one term in Congress from 1903 to 1905. Disston did not run for office, but he financially backed many Republican candidates at all levels, and he was a prominent political advisor who was well known on a national level. Let's look closer at the careers of both men.

George Shiras III
Hunting Wild Life with Camera and Flashlight

George Shiras was a prolific photographer, and his family had sufficient resources that he could afford to spend a great deal of time in the field stalking wild game with his camera. By the early 1900s he had assembled an impressive portfolio of prints, many of which were taken at night, using a blast of magnesium flash powder to illuminate the subject.

In 1905, while serving in Congress, Shiras visited Gilbert Grosvenor at the National Geographic Society office in Washington and showed him a portfolio of prints. Grosvenor, the editor of the society's magazine, was immediately taken by the stark beauty and drama of the photographs and told Shiras he wanted to publish them. Grosvenor had just published the magazine's first photographs – eleven images taken in Tibet – but after seeing Shiras's work Grosvenor decided to devote an entire issue of the magazine to his photographs.

Seventy-four of Shiras's photographs appeared in the July 1906 issue, with very little text, and the reaction was swift, and varied. The public loved the issue, which the magazine had to reprint to meet demand, and membership in the society swelled. The society's board, however, was not so enamored. Some felt that publishing a journal filled with photographs did not reflect the society's high-minded mission of "diffusing geographic knowledge." Two members of the board resigned in disgust, objecting that their journal had been relegated to a "picture book."

Grosvenor feared for his job, but apparently the flood of membership checks convinced his bosses that there was a future in publishing wildlife photography. Grosvenor and Shiras worked together many more times, Shiras was elected to the society's board in 1911, and in 1935 *National Geographic* published Shiras's two-volume classic, *Hunting Wild Life with Camera and Flashlight*.

Shiras joined the Revels Island Club in 1894 and built a large, two-storied frame dwelling with a wide front porch and stone fireplaces. The home also included a photographic darkroom, where Shiras would develop the photos taken on his daily outings.

Hunting Wild Life with Camera and Flashlight includes two chapters on Shiras's Revels Island days, along with 42 photographs taken on the island. These chapters provide important documentation of what life was like in the hunting clubs that proliferated along the coast in the late 1800s and early 1900s and are now gone. Periodicals of the day frequently included articles about visits to gunning clubs and island hotels, and these can be found in various online archives. But here we have an account written by a club member, documented with his own photographs, which were developed in a darkroom in his island home.

Shiras was a part time resident of Revels Island for nearly forty years, and his accounts in *Hunting Wild Life* reflect his strong commitment to conservation as well as his growing interest in photography. Shiras was only 25 when he began spending time on Revels Island, but he was concerned then that activities such as spring shorebird shooting were not sustainable and would eventually prove harmful to wildlife. Shiras noticed in his early days on the island that shorebird numbers already were dwindling, and he described shorebird shooting as wholesale slaughter and a wasteful practice:

> It is not strange that eventually a tremendous decrease in shorebirds was observed during migrations, for in the spring when the local shorebirds were either nesting or mating, every clubhouse from Virginia to New Jersey was filled with members intent on hunting shorebirds at a season when all other shooting was prohibited. Day after day, I have seen otherwise reputable sportsmen bring in 200 birds, and when the weather was warm it was practically impossible to keep such birds from spoiling.

Shiras traveled a great deal but clearly enjoyed escaping to the quiet and solitude of Revels Island:

> Like many other members of the Revels Island club, in the middle nineties, I visited the shore in the spring not so much for shooting at a time when other game was protected as for enjoying the beauty of Nature throwing off her drab winter garment and replacing it with green, swelling buds and unfolding leaves. This beauty, the gentle warmth of the sun, and the soft spring breezes constituted a welcome change to the residents of more northern latitudes who loved the out-of-doors.

In addition to the wild landscape, Shiras seemed to enjoy the people of Revels Island. He wrote little about fellow club members and guests, but he greatly appreciated the skills of the guides, and especially those of Aunt Caroline, the longtime manager of the club kitchen:

> Aunt Caroline, a faithful and proficient colored cook, had charge of the club kitchen for more than a generation. Living in a State famous for its culinary art, she had few equals. The making of delicious clam chowder was one of her greatest accomplishments, and large clams were always available on a sandspit only about 100 yards away.
>
> Early in the fall a goodly supply of oysters would be gathered from distant bays and placed in the shallow water on both sides of a long dock. Sometimes between meals a guide would wade out and get a basketful of them, which would be opened and eaten by us on the sunny side of the boathouse. Aunt Caroline served the oysters in several ways.
>
> In winter months, eels speared in their hibernating places in the mud at the heads of creeks were another delicacy on the bill of fare. In the hunting season Aunt Caroline produced the most appetizing dishes of perfectly cooked ducks and shore birds, besides stewed terrapin and snipe potpies. The memory of her pastries, including apple and pumpkin pies, puddings, doughnuts, and other tasty products of her skill, still remains with me. Even the little tin lunch pails that were sent out to the blinds with us were like little Christmas boxes with their varied assortment of good things to allay the hearty appetites we had sharpened by hours in the open air.

Shiras's final visit to Revels Island came in May 1923 when he was accompanied by his friend, Dr. E.W. Nelson, Chief of the U.S. Biological Survey. The visit, wrote Shiras, was to assess the effectiveness of the migratory bird laws passed in 1916 and 1918. "The launch had no sooner put out from the little port town of Wachapreague, than Hudsonian curlews (whimbrels) began springing up on all sides and we observed nearly a thousand on the six-mile trip. Yet, this bird had nearly become extinct ten years before," wrote Shiras.

Shiras and Nelson spent several days exploring the salt marshes and tidal flats of Revels Island and discovered that the populations of knots, willets, dunlins, plovers, dowitchers, turnstones, and sandpipers had indeed responded well to the conservation laws. The lone exception was the yellowlegs, which Shiras said could still be legally hunted. Additional legislation was passed in 1927 closing the season on yellowlegs.

And so, in his lifetime, George Shiras 3d accomplished three significant firsts. He became America's first real wildlife photographer, putting together an amazing collection of action pictures of birds and mammals going about their daily and nightly business. He recognized the folly of allowing shorebirds to be killed as they were mating and nesting, and he was among the first to persuade Congress to outlaw the practice. And, last but not least, he was the first to have a cover-to-cover photo spread in *National Geographic* magazine.

George Shiras died at age 83 on March 24, 1942 in Marquette, on Michigan's Upper Peninsula, where his family had owned land for many years. The Shiras family maintained homes in Marquette, where they spent their summers, in Ormond Beach, Florida, where they spent their winters, and in Pittsburgh, where they did business. Shiras kept his island getaway on the Eastern Shore for nearly 40 years, and it must have been a therapeutic retreat for him. It was a place where he could escape business and politics for a few weeks, using his camera to document nesting terns and skimmers, spending his evenings developing film and making prints in his darkroom.

Hamilton Disston
Draining the Swamp

Hamilton Disston was born in Philadelphia on August 23, 1844. His father, Henry Disston, was an English immigrant whose father died shortly after arriving in the United States. Henry was a toolmaker and machinist who founded a company that made industrial saw blades, files, and hacksaws. Henry held numerous patents, and his company, Henry Disston and Sons, grew quickly as northern industries flourished in the years following the American Civil War. Henry built a steel mill in the Philadelphia suburb of Tacony, eventually employing more than 2,000 people. By the 1870s the company was one of the largest suppliers of industrial blades in the world, with an annual production of 1.4 million hacksaws and 3 million files.

Hamilton attended public schools in Philadelphia until he was 15, then went to work as an apprentice in the steel mill. When his father died in 1878 Hamilton and his brothers inherited the business. Hamilton, the eldest brother, became the controlling partner.

With the steel business growing, Hamilton began investing in other ventures, mainly real estate in Atlantic City, New Jersey, and other locations along the coast. Hamilton was an avid sport fisherman, and in 1877 Henry Sanford, founder of the town of Sanford, Florida, and former diplomat to Belgium, invited him to visit Florida for some fishing. While exploring the lakes, rivers, and vast swamplands of south Florida, Hamilton realized that huge tracts of land might possibly be converted to agriculture by diverting rivers and draining Lake Okeechobee, Florida's largest freshwater lake.

In the 1840s and 1850s the state of Florida was given grants by Congress to reclaim some 15 million acres of swampland by constructing canals and levees. Florida also received grants to build rail infrastructure to encourage settlement in the southern portion of the state. The drainage funds and the railroad funds were consolidated in a trust called the Internal Improvement Fund of the State of Florida. This fund underwrote bonds issued by railroad companies to help finance construction, but the great costs associated with the Civil War and Reconstruction caused the railroad companies to default on the bonds, thus depleting the trust. By 1877 the trust was deeply in debt and facing foreclosure.

After Disston's fishing trip in 1877, he began negotiating with Florida officials to help the state relieve its debt, revive the effort to convert wetlands to agricultural land, and extend railroad infrastructure down the east coast. In 1881 Disston and the state of Florida agreed to a contract that would pay Florida $1 million in exchange for four million acres of land held in the Internal Improvement Fund. In effect, Disston was purchasing four million acres of Florida land at twenty-five cents per acre.

Disston signed the contract on June 14, 1881, and the *New York Times* declared it "the largest purchase of land ever made by a single person in the world." Disston became the largest landowner in the United States. Now, all he had to do was drain the swamp.

Disston began with a massive dredging project to drain the Kissimmee flood plain that flows into Lake Okeechobee. Canals were dug to divert overflow from Okeechobee into the St. Lucie River, and thence to the Atlantic Ocean. The Caloosahatchee overflow would be diverted into the Gulf of Mexico, and the Everglades would be drained by a system of canals that would move the water south to the coast.

At first, it seemed to work. A June 1883 report indicated that the Kissimmee flood plain was drying up, just as Disston had planned. The project also generated national publicity for the state of Florida. In the four years after Disston's purchase, railroad infrastructure increased four times over what it had in the past twenty years. Land sales multiplied six times, and the state's taxable property inventory doubled. More than 150,000 tourists visited Florida during the winter of 1884.

Disston built a huge sugar plantation and opened real estate offices across the United States and Europe, promoting low-cost land in sunny Florida. This drew many people to Orlando, and it sparked the development of cities such as Sarasota, Naples, and Tarpon Springs. Disston headquartered his Caloosahatchee project in Fort Myers and began developing land in the Tampa area.

The project also drew the attention of railroad magnate Henry Flagler, who vacationed in St. Augustine in the early 1880s and built a magnificent hotel there. Flagler, the founder of Standard Oil, was also the founder of the Florida East Coast Railway, which would eventually reach Daytona, Miami, and Palm Beach.

Disston's project to drain Florida's vast swamplands was a great success in that it sparked a national bull market for Florida real estate. It replenished the coffers of the state's Internal Improvement Fund, and it brought investors from the north who spent millions in the cities and towns of south Florida. But the number of acres reclaimed from swampland were minimal, and the costs were devastatingly high.

Lake Okeechobee, which naturally rises and falls with rainfall, was not affected by Disston's canals. The 1883 report that the Kissimmee valley was drying up turned out to be in error. A drought had caused the water level to fall. Still, south Florida had been transformed. The railroad ran south to Miami and Palm Beach, and west to Tampa. There were hotels and orange groves and beach resorts, and they came not because Hamilton Disston successfully drained the swamps, but simply because he had made the well-publicized attempt.

Hamilton Disston remained in Florida for a few years, and returned to Pennsylvania in the early 1890s. In 1893 a serious recession affected every sector of the American economy and created political upheaval. Disston mortgaged his Florida assets for $2 million and returned to the steel mill. On April 30, 1896 Disston and his wife had dinner with the mayor of Philadelphia and attended a theatre presentation. The next morning, he was found dead. Some reports say that he committed suicide, using a handgun to end his life. Others say he died of natural causes, a heart attack. The official determination, performed by the coroner, was that Disston died of heart failure.

Hamilton Disston spent a great deal of time among the Virginia barrier islands, but it is not known whether he owned property. He and George Shiras, two Pennsylvania Republicans, form a link. An article in the September 22, 1887 issue of *Forest & Stream* magazine gives this somewhat cryptic report on the Accomac and Revels Island Clubs: "There are two clubs in the county now; one of the Accomac Club some twenty members, about four miles down the river. The other is at Revels Island has some one hundred members, I believe, from all parts of the country. It is very inaccessible, being a long sail to it. Mr. Hamilton Disston, of Philadelphia, owns, I think, several shares in it, and his steam yacht *Manatee* is a frequent visitor to our waters for shooting and fishing."

Disston may or may not have been a member of the Revels Island Club, but the *Manatee* served as his private gunning club afloat. He was often seen on the seaside, usually in either Chincoteague or Wachapreague, and he usually had a gaggle of Pennsylvania politicians with him. He visited with a group in the spring of 1881 to go shorebird shooting, and *The Democratic Messenger* of Snow Hill had this item in its May 14 edition:

"Mr. Hamilton Disston, the well-known saw manufacturer, accompanied by a number of Philadelphia politicians, arrived in his steam pleasure yacht at Chincoteague Island one day this week. They have been killing from 500 to 1,000 birds a day, since their arrival."

Disston was well known on the national political scene in the 1880s, and he enjoyed a bit of celebrity on the Eastern Shore. Harness racing was a popular sport at the time, and Alfred S. Kellam, proprietor of the Powellton Hotel in what would become Wachapreague, named his race horse in honor of the Pennsylvania Republican. Hamilton Disston, the race horse, apparently distinguished himself at tracks on and off the Shore, and eventually was banned from entering local races because he soundly dominated other competitors. In advertisements for racing events, Hamilton Disston would be listed as an attendant, but would not compete.

Alfred Kellam, the owner of the horse, no doubt took delight in publishing advertisements in the *Peninsula Enterprise* each spring announcing that Hamilton Disston would be available for stud services at Kellam's farm near Keller.

Disston has a link with another man who indirectly has had a profound influence on the islands. That man is Henry Flagler, the railroad magnate who followed Disston's lead and developed the east coast of Florida. In the early 1970s, when the Virginia islands were threatened with development, The Nature Conservancy moved to limit the development by purchasing the adjacent islands. The funds to do so were provided by the Mary Flagler Cary Charitable Trust of New York. Mary Flagler Cary was the granddaughter of Henry Flagler. Over the years, the Cary Trust has invested some $20 million in conservation efforts on the Eastern Shore.

Chapter 7:
The Accomac Club

The most lavish island getaway was the Accomac Club, built on a high marsh on the north end of Parramore Island, east of Wachapreague. The club was chartered on January 12, 1887 and was originally limited to 35 members. To become a member, an applicant had to be approved by a unanimous vote of existing members, pay an initiation fee of $100, and then pay annual dues of $75. Most of the members were businessmen from New York City.

The curious thing about the Accomac Club is its connection to the Fulton Fish Market in New York, which was built in 1822 beneath what is now the base of the Brooklyn Bridge on the East River. The seven men who founded the Accomac Club were involved with the Fulton Market, and several of the members were officers of both the market and the club. In the 1890s Samuel Stoner was president of the club. He also was president of the Fulton Fish Market. Benjamin West also served as president of the club in the 1890s. He was secretary of the Fulton Fish Market.

Another curious aspect about the club is the way it fully embraced the Eastern Shore community. Most of the gunning clubs employed local people as guides, cooks, and caretakers, but the Accomac Club went to great lengths to ingratiate itself with the people and the government of Accomack County.

Each May, around the time we celebrate Memorial Day today, the club would hold a regatta in which local sailors would compete for prizes such as silver tea sets, gold pieces, parlor clocks, and sewing machines. The regattas attracted hundreds of people to the seaside east of Wachapreague, and a great banquet would be held and speeches would be made. Officers of the club would eloquently sing the praises of Accomack County, and local dignitaries would extend a warm welcome to their northern friends. Music would be part of the celebration, and the Cashville Cornet Band was a favorite.

The spring regatta was a special social occasion for Accomack County, and the local newspapers gave full coverage to both the sailboat races and the celebrations that attended them. The *Peninsula Enterprise* of Accomac reported in its June 6, 1891 edition:

> The regatta given by the Accomac Club came off as announced, on the 1st inst., at Wachapreague Inlet and was attended by several hundred persons, among them many ladies, who witnessed the races from the balcony of the club house. Perfect order prevailed and the kindliest feelings pervaded the immense assemblage during the entire day. Promptly at 10 a.m., Mr. Crook, the genial and eloquent secretary, presented on behalf of the club four very valuable silver trophies, purchased for the occasion at a cost of $300, and two gold coins of $5 each, to A.S. Kellam, Esq., Capts. Asa Savage and Newell Rich, the special committee in charge of the regatta, in which he stated among other things, that the club wished to promote good feeling and exchange courtesies with the people of "Old Virginny," and that having donated the prizes the responsibility rested with the special committee, that the prizes given were results of the uniform kindness of the citizens towards members of the club, who had selected its site because of proverbial Virginia hospitality and if the day's races proved a success, future contests on a much larger and grander scale would follow, which was received with hearty and prolonged cheers for the Accomac Club."

The races were run from the clubhouse to Sandy Point and back, a distance of about four miles. Boats were divided into classes of 11, 13, 16, and 18 feet, and there were two winners in each class, who took home silver trophies and gold coins. The overall winner of the day was

Thomas B. Smith, sailing an 18-footer, who finished the course in a time of 45 minutes. He won a gold piece.

Reported the *Peninsula Enterprise*:

> The races completed, all returned to the Club-house, where a sumptuous and elegant dinner, furnished by the Club, was spread, and where costly Madieras, Hollands, Cognacs and lager flowed as from a living foundation, of which not a few freely partook, while all went as merry as a marriage bell. Feasting and convivialities over, the next to follow was the presentation of the prizes to the winners by Hon. A. Crook of the Club, who in his usual dignified and impressive manner, delivered one of the most beautiful and thrilling addresses to the winners to the citizens of Accomac, that your humble correspondent has had the pleasure of hearing lo these many years. It was received with the long and hearty applause, justly merited.
>
> Geo. F. Parramore, Esq., of the Accomac bar, responded in behalf of the winners and the citizens of the county, in a felicitous and forcible speech that carried conviction to the hearts of all present that he was the right man in the right place and equal to the occasion in every respect, which was followed by prolonged cheers and lively singing participated in by most of the large assemblage of ladies and gentlemen present, followed by a general handshaking and homeward departure. Every member of the Club present, about a dozen, tried to excel the others in receiving and entertaining all visitors.
>
> To your correspondent a notice of the Club, in this connection, seems to be singularly appropriate – and any mention made of the liberal, courteous and high-toned gentlemen composing it, can hardly fail to interest the readers of the *Enterprise*. Organized in 1887 with seven members, it now has the limited membership of 35, consisting of New York business and professional men of abundant means, many of them being millionaires. The property of the Club has been improved yearly and they now have an elegant two-story building about 30x50 feet, with all modern improvements and conveniences therein, large porches around same, an annex about 20 X 24 feet, a detached dining room, cook house, boat house, provision and ice house, garden, a miniature palace known as Eddy's Retreat, a fast and handsome yacht "Challenge," several batteaux and gunning boats of all description.

In addition to the improvements above enumerated, the Club proposes to have erected soon a two-story annex 40x25 ft., the lower floor to be used as a billiard and ball room and the upper as a parlor and 8 private bed rooms – also a boat house 75x25 ft., in which they will house their boats. They are having an elegant steam-yacht built, which will be completed in a few months and used to convey them to and from Wachapreague and about the waters adjacent thereto. All the members being gentlemen of leisure they make frequent visits for pleasure only and eat whatever game they chance to kill, never shipping for market or otherwise disposing of their birds.

The genial and clever secretary informed the visitors, that the Club expended on an average not less than $5000 annually, in Accomac, which went directly into the pockets of their resident employees, the merchants, liverymen, etc,. and that nothing used by them was bought outside of Accomac, except their cigars and wines, which could not be purchased here.

The following personal mention of some of the members will be of interest to the readers of the *Enterprise*.

B.W. West, president, is secretary of the Fulton Market Fishmongers Association, N.Y. – the ruling leader of the Club – genial and a ladies' admirer – an "old timer" in every way.

S.L. Stoner, vice-president, is president of the same Association – has sweet tenor voice – hard to start and equally hard to stop – never loses a meal – always sacrifices himself for others.

Abel Crook, lawyer, New York City -- very successful secretary and treasurer -- carries the finances and insists upon reciprocity between members and citizens of Virginia -- nicknamed "Christopher Columbus."

Eddy, retired merchant, nicknamed by Club "Commodore" -- always obliging to everyone -- has at his own expense erected a necessary adjunct, designated "Eddy's Retreat."

C. W. Wingert -- speculator in most anything -- nicknamed "Jowls," because of his wonderful appetite and disposition to grunt at slight provocation, from which he quickly recovered -- he is a noted wing shot, some people say, that suggested his name "Wing-gert."

P. Kelley is the great clam-finder and opener -- his record for beer drinking has led to his nickname of "Bad Boy" -- he was never known to find fault, and in time will probably kill a bird or two.

H.M. Rogers, nicknamed the "Chaplain," weight 360 pounds -- prefers to sit still and shoot from a hard marsh "Calico-backs," and always contented -- is reckoned a champion at snoring.

L.D. Duryea, manufacturer -- the youngest member of the Club -- unassuming in manners, upright in character -- lives not for himself alone but for the mutual pleasure of all his friends -- a good shot and passionately fond of all out-door sports -- nicknamed by the Club "Starchy."

Henry Spratley, railroad president -- on his virgin visit after a membership of two years -- after rising at 3 a. m., June 1st, went out shooting and remarked, he had "caught on" and had the "shooting disease" -- in every way a good fellow -- a good judge of cigars which his friends take with appreciation -- prescribes pleasant and successful remedies for member's aches and pains -- nicknamed the "Doctor."

Absence of the other members at regatta accounts for want of mention. As a whole their reputation is one of which they may well be proud.

Capt. Chas. A. Delano, is steward of the Club, which is open the year round. He is an excellent cook and always welcomes in the name of the Club all who visit the property, whether members or citizens of the State of Virginia.

The motto of the Club is, "Open to all Gentlemen. The latch string is on the outside and none need go hungry or thirsty who may stop at their door." "All are Welcome."

This curiously felicitous relationship between New York City businessmen and Accomack County farmers and fishermen could be explained by noting that these folks had a strong common interest. The Eastern Shore was one of the most productive seafood sources on the East Coast in the 1890s, sending to northern markets thousands of gallons of oysters, as well as diamondback terrapins, which were extremely valuable and highly sought by restaurants.

Polk Lang, a local ship captain and businessman, had an oyster shucking house on Folly Creek that employed more than fifty shuckers during the season. Could it be that the regattas, the valuable prizes, the banquets, and the welcoming nature of the club were designed to foster a close relationship with important suppliers of seafood for the Fulton Market?

The men who ran the club surely had a close relationship with Eastern Shore fishermen, seafood dealers, and brokers. A newspaper story covering a regatta in the 1890s listed Capt. Polk Lang of Folly Creek among the winners. He received a silver pitcher for his first place finish.

The end of the Accomac Club, like many of the old clubs and hotels on the barrier islands, came with the August 1933 hurricane, which did major damage. But in reality, the club was treading water long before the 1933 storm. While other clubs were done in by an eroding landscape, the Accomac Club was done in by the eroding fortunes of its members. The Great Depression took its toll long before the storm. A letter from club member Walter A. Heath to his friend Hal Lovell in late 1933 indicated that membership was down to "six or seven men" by the time the storm struck.

Chapter 8:
Parramore Island

In 1969, when the Smith Island Development Corporation of New York announced plans for a massive resort and second home community on Smith, Myrtle, and Ship Shoal Islands, The Nature Conservancy quickly bought neighboring Godwin Island in an effort to block the developer's plans. TNC ownership, combined with passage of legislation in the Virginia General Assembly to protect coastal waters and wetlands, ended the project.

Today, The Nature Conservancy is one of the world's largest conservation organizations, with an annual budget of more than a billion dollars and projects that span the globe. But in 1969 few people had even heard of it. TNC had few members, a modest budget, and a small staff working out of a suite of offices in Arlington, Virginia.

Few people on the Eastern Shore knew anything about TNC but TNC knew a lot about the Eastern Shore. TNC had been keeping an eye on the peninsula for years, beginning in 1955 when the United States Navy announced plans to take Parramore Island by condemnation and use the island for bombing practice by its aviators.

The Nature Conservancy was aware that the Virginia coast was home to a chain of uninhabited barrier islands, a fragile ecosystem rare because of its pristine, unaltered state, and also because of its size. The string of islands extended nearly 100 miles from the Virginia capes northward into Maryland. You just don't find intact coastal ecosystems like that.

In 1955 TNC was in its infant stage. The story that TNC began with five scientists sitting around the kitchen table talking about ways to save the planet was not far from the truth. When the navy cast a covetous eye toward Parramore Island, it gave those five scientists something to focus on, a project that offered drama and immediacy. It was David versus Goliath, the military/industrial complex versus a rural and unspoiled area of incomparable beauty.

On January 20, 1955 the *Peninsula Enterprise*, a weekly newspaper published in Accomac, broke the story that the navy was planning to take the island and use it as a bombing range. Such military use of the islands was not unprecedented. The islands had been used for target practice during World War II, and more recently the air force had been using Wreck Island to test live ordnance. But the Parramore proposal touched a number of sensitive issues, ranging from the health of the local economy to the need to protect the natural landscape.

According to newspaper accounts, the plan was opposed by the chamber of commerce and by watermen's groups because of the potential for damage to oyster beds and the recreational fishing industry in Wachapreague and Quinby. Conservationists opposed the plan because it would have caused irreparable damage to one of the largest and most pristine maritime forests in the coastal chain.

Establishment of a bombing range would have required clearing two 6,000-foot diameter target areas, meaning virtual destruction of the maritime forest in the island's interior. Other than Assateague, Parramore was the only barrier island remaining with a significant stand of old-growth forest.

Meanwhile, while the project was being sorted out in the news media, the owners of the island contacted George B. Fell, TNC's executive director, and asked for help. The owners, Mrs. Jean Saunders of Cincinnati, Ohio, and her son, Dr. Carl Schmidlapp of Glen Cove, New York, were conservationists who understood the degree of devastation the project would bring. In February 1955 TNC was approached by Richard Hollerith, a friend of the Schmidlapps, who had recently moved to Warwick, a colonial era plantation near Quinby. Mr.

Hollerith met with George Fell, and TNC promised to join with the Schmidlapp family in the effort to protect the island.

In those days, TNC had few members, no national recognition, and a very limited budget. George Fell's position of executive director at that time was unpaid. Protection efforts were grassroot, mainly a letter writing campaign and an effort to rally other conservation organizations and influential individuals. TNC's interest was in protecting Parramore and other islands as wilderness area, as opposed to conveying them to the National Park Service for public recreation.

The navy's interest eventually cooled, the project was dropped, and other matters provided the headlines in the local newspapers. But the seeds had been planted, the lamp had been lighted. A relationship had begun between TNC and the Schmidlapp family that would last for years. And TNC had launched a revolutionary new game plan when it came to protecting landscapes and the natural communities they support. You buy them, you set up a team to manage them, and you do it over and over again.

Nearly twenty years would pass before TNC would become the owner of Parramore Island. The Schmidlapp family and TNC began a lengthy courtship, one whose outcome was foreshadowed and predictable, yet slow to be consummated. The Schmidlapps were conservationists and outdoor folks who wanted to see their island protected in the long term. But they also enjoyed spending time on Parramore, where they converted the abandoned life-saving station to an island getaway for family and friends.

TNC's mission was to find a way for the Schmidlapps to enjoy their island and still protect it. Dr. Richard H. Goodwin, TNC's president, contacted Dr. Schmidlapp in 1957 and suggested that the family donate a portion of the island each year. Dr. Schmidlapp replied that his attorneys recommended against the plan, but he emphasized that he would one day like to see TNC acquire the island.

In late 1969, when the Smith Island Development Corporation announced its plan to build a $150 million resort community of 40,000 to 50,000 people, it created a sense of urgency. In February 1970 the

New York Times published an article predicting the growing likelihood of intense commercial development of the Virginia barrier islands, the last chain of islands along the mid-Atlantic yet to be developed.

TNC leadership, meanwhile, found a partner willing to work with them on the new approach of land conservation through purchase and management. The Mary Flagler Cary Charitable Trust made it possible for TNC to create the Virginia Coast Reserve, which over a decade grew to a 45,000-acre preserve containing fourteen islands, vast seaside salt meadows, and contiguous upland.

Backed by the financial resources of the Cary Trust, in 1970 TNC bought Godwin Island, Metompkin Island, a large part of Hog, and Smith, Myrtle, and Ship Shoal, the group slated for development. With the fire extinguished, TNC again returned its attention to the Schmidlapps and Parramore.

On June 2, 1971, representatives of TNC met with Dr. Schmidlapp and other stockholders of the Parramore Island Corporation. The stockholders had agreed that a sale would hinge upon three factors: the land must remain in its natural state, the corporation members must have use of the island for twenty years, and a sale must generate a satisfactory return for the stockholders. It was agreed to have an independent appraisal made.

An appraisal was made during the fall, and contact was made with the Cary Trust regarding the possibility of funding a purchase. In April 1972 TNC vice president Pat Noonan met with principals of the corporation to discuss key provisions of an agreement.

In April 1973 the TNC Board of Governors approved a purchase agreement that would convey the island to TNC. The Schmidlapp group would have rights to the island for twenty years. The Cary Trust agreed to fund the project at $1.6 million.

The Parramore purchase was not one of the first made by TNC, but it was the most significant because the island had the largest maritime forest remaining in the chain. It was the "crown jewel," said the newspaper headlines.

And it happened because the U.S. Navy, in 1955, decided that the island would make a good place to train aviators in the art of dropping bombs.

The Parramore Family

The Parramores were a distinguished Eastern Shore family that lived on a seaside plantation called Bellevue, north and west of the island that bears their name. Parramores fought in the American Revolution and later served the community as judges, doctors, and elected officials. The island came into the family through marriage.

According to Ralph T. Whitelaw's history of the Eastern Shore, the patent for 800 acres on what was then called "Feaks His Island" went to William Custis in 1686. The following year, an additional 100 acres went to Isaac Metcalf. When William Custis died in 1721, he left his part of the island to his granddaughter, Joanna Custis Hope, who married Thomas Parramore. The Parramores bought Isaac Metcalf's holdings from his heirs, and thereby owned the island in its entirety. The island then took on the name of the owners.

The first Parramore came to America as an indentured servant, but by the time of the Revolution the family was among the leaders of the growing Virginia colony. John Parramore arrived in 1622 aboard the *Bona Venture* as a 17-year old servant to John Blower. By the 1630s Parramore's name was appearing regularly in court documents, ranging in nature from litigation over business transactions to a charge of cursing on the Sabbath. By the early 1640s, Parramore was thriving to the point where he had an indentured servant of his own, Edward Robins.

By 1650 Parramore was living on a 200-acre plantation in Northampton County on Magothy Bay. He later bought a 250-acre farm on Occohannock Creek on the Chesapeake Bay. On November 9, 1666, Parramore patented 1,500 acres in northern Accomack County near the Maryland line, and then had to repeat the patent process with Maryand in 1668 when Virginia gave up its claim to the area. Parramore thus named the plantation "Double Purchase." He died there in 1676.

Thomas Parramore, a grandson of John, married the widow Joanna Custis Hope, granddaughter of William Custis, younger brother of Major General John Custis. Joanna inherited the Bellevue land, including what would become Parramore Island, from her grandfather.

Thomas survived Joanna and when he died in 1774 left Bellevue to his son William, "my heir apparent." A second son, John, was given the land in Maryland, and Thomas, the third son, was bequeathed the property in Northampton County.

William was a prominent man in the community and in 1777 was one of the justices who transferred allegiance from the Crown to the Commonwealth of Virginia. He was a colonel of the militia in the Revolution and in the years following the war converted to Methodism and became a deeply religious man who grew to detest slavery. In 1787 he issued a deed of manumission freeing his ten slaves: "I, William Parramore, being fully convinced of the just and equal right that all human nature have to the happy enjoyment of personal liberty, as well as that the slavery of our fellow creatures is repugnant to and a violation of our blessed Christian religion, have and hereby do manumit, set free, and discharge my several negro slaves..."

The Parramore family served its community and country with distinction. Thomas Parramore was first elected to the House of Burgesses in 1748 and reelected thirteen times before his death in the 1770s. His oldest son, William, was an Accomack County justice and a trustee of Garrison's Chapel when it was built in 1787. William's son, Thomas, was a colonel in the Revolutionary army.

Four Parramores served in the Virginia legislature, beginning with Thomas' tenure of some twenty-five years in the House of Burgesses until the end of the Civil War. Thomas Custis Parramore was a member of the House during that war, and he became judge of the county court in 1870. William Parramore was a physician who practiced in Accomac in the 1880s.

The Custis and Parramore families owned Parramore Island from the patent date of 1686 until Parramore heirs sold it in 1871 to Talmadge F. Cherry of Baltimore. It changed hands several more times before being purchased in 1892 by the Parramore Land and Improvement Company. It was at this point that Parramore Island had its first brush with becoming a resort property.

The Parramore Land and Improvement Company was chartered in February 1892, and its stockholders were Pennsylvania Railroad executives. Its president was Joseph L Ferrell, president of the Broadwater Land and Improvement Company on neighboring Hog Island and host of President Grover Cleveland when he came for hunting and fishing trips. According to the charter, the mission of the company was to "build thereon, dwelling houses, stores and pleasure resorts, to establish wharves, to promote the farming, grazing and hunting facilities of the same, &c." Seven men were listed as stockholders, and all but one gave Philadelphia as his home address. Ferrell listed Broadwater, Northampton County, as his home.

The 1892 attempt to develop Parramore had much in common with the attempt by the Smith Island Development Corporation in 1969. Both suffered from terrible timing. In 1969 people were beginning to realize that coastal wetlands are an important part of the landscape, the natural source of wonderful things such as fish, clams, and oysters. Federal and state legislators sensed this changing attitude and were passing laws to protect wetlands. The Smith Island company was launching into the teeth of a gale.

For the Parramore Land and Improvement Company, the worst financial depression of the post-Civil War era was hovering on the distant horizon. The Panic of 1893 brought business and industry to a standstill, and especially hard hit was the railroad industry, whose infrastructure was rotting and falling apart. Railroads went into receivership, 15,000 businesses went bankrupt, and 640 banks failed. The Panic of 1893 brought about "the complete unsettlement of confidence and the derangement of our financial machinery...and had the effect of stopping the wheels of industry...," reported the *Commercial and Financial Chronicle*.

The Panic of 1893 extended into 1894 and 1895, and the railroad executives' dream of a resort on Parramore Island did not come to fruition. The island changed hands several times, and a private gunning club operated on the island until it was damaged in the 1933 storm. A few years later it was purchased by the Schmidlapp family.

The Parramore story ends with a bit of irony. Funds to purchase the island, and others in the chain, came from the Mary Flagler Cary Charitable Trust. Mary Flagler Cary was the granddaughter of Henry Flagler, one of the founders and principal owners of Standard Oil. Henry Flagler was also one of the principal developers of Florida's east coast. Flagler vacationed in St. Augustine in the early 1880s and built a magnificent hotel there. He founded the Florida East Coast Railway, which would eventually transform Florida's ocean beaches into the resort cities of Daytona, Miami, and Palm Beach.

So, the fortune accumulated by a man who in his lifetime developed miles of ocean beach, would, a century later, be used to protect a pristine coastal wilderness in Virginia.

Chapter 9:
Hog Island

Most of Virginia's barrier islands have been populated by transients. People stayed in hotels and gunning clubs, they came to celebrate pony roundups, they fished or enjoyed a day at the beach, they worked for a while at a life-saving station. And then they left.

But Hog Island was made up of Eastern Shore people. They were residents whose roots went back generations. They were part of us, related if not by blood, then certainly in spirit. My family's roots go back to Red Bank Landing, where my great-grandfather John had a farm and operated a small shipping business. When he looked to the east, he saw Hog Island. When a Hog Islander looked to the west, he saw John's farm. They were the same people, just with different views.

Hog Island, and to a lesser extent Assateague, was not just an island, but a town, a community of people whose lives and families were intertwined. Hog Island was populated by more than 100 people, Assateague by about two dozen. Hog Island had its share of transients, too. There were vacation cottages and a gunning club, whose members primarily were railroad executives. President-elect Grover Cleveland came for an extended stay in 1892, prior to beginning his second term, putting the island on the front page of newspapers all across the country.

The transients left in the 1920s, their fortunes ebbing with the

Great Depression like a tidal creek at full moon. And then came the storm of 1933, which overwashed the island and flattened the dunes and floated the coffins out of the cemetery, and so began the great exodus of the Hog Islanders. They jacked up their houses, placed pine logs beneath them, hitched them up to a team of mules, and rolled them onto the decks of oyster monitors. Hog Island homes were towed everywhere from Willis Wharf to Chincoteague, where they were placed on foundations on higher land. The Methodist church ended up in Oyster. The last man standing on Hog Island was said to have been Southey "Sud" Bell, a tall, lanky fellow known for picking the banjo at the Red Onion, Hog Island's gathering spot.

There still are a few people around who remember life on Hog Island, but the number dwindles with each passing year. Fortunately, a few wrote about their experiences on the island, and the Eastern Shore Barrier Islands Center produced a film called *My Island Home*, which featured three people who had been born on Hog Island. One of them, Yvonne Marshall Wigeon, wrote a small book in 1988 called *Precious Memories of Childhood Days on Hog Island*. In the introduction she wrote, "One of my fondest childhood memories was listening to my mother tell about her childhood on Hog Island. Even after I grew up I could still spend hours listening to my mother and my aunts tell and retell stories of 'the good ol'days' when they were young girls. It was during one of these 'tale telling' sessions that it occurred to me that these ladies were of the last generation of Hog Islanders who could tell firsthand how it was 75-80 years ago on the island. It was then that I decided I wanted these stories kept alive...."

L.E. Doughty grew up on Hog Island and lived there until his family moved to New Jersey around 1923. He wrote a book called *A Narrative About Life on Hog Island, Va.*, which presents a straightforward, unsentimental account of what it was like to live and work on the island during the early days of the 20th century.

The last days of Hog Island have been well documented. The early days are something of a mystery. Charles A. Sterling, the lighthouse keeper, wrote a small book in 1903 called simply *Hog Island Virginia*, and in it he speculates that the first residents were a group of twenty-five colonists who received a patent for the island but mysteriously disappeared, much in the manner of the Lost Colony of North Carolina. According to Sterling, there was a document in the state capital in Richmond dated 1672 "which consists of a 'letter paten' to Sir Henry Chimchley, of the islands known as Machipongo, and his grant of the same to certain Colonists..." Here Sterling lists the names of the twenty-five men and women, none of whom had familiar Hog Island surnames.

Sterling's theory is that the settlers were massacred by "the warlike tribes of the Accomacs, who would not be likely to submit to having their most fruitful isle seized, like the brightest jewel torn from a crown."

Sterling posited that "The Indians may have closed in upon the island with a great fleet of canoes and massacred and tortured or slain the last one of the settlers; or the mosquitos may have routed the Colony; but if they left the island of their own accord some of them would undoubtedly have remained in the vicinity. But there is not one of their descendants on the Atlantic coast today. There is not the slightest clew to the fate of these people..."

It makes a good story, but the local Indians were not known to have been warlike. In fact, most accounts during the early contact period depict the native people as friendly, generous, and somewhat meek. In addition, local natives were semi-nomadic, and although they did visit the islands for hunting and fishing forays, most lived on the mainland where there was more room to roam. Sterling might have had a valid point about the mosquitos, though.

Ralph T. Whitelaw, in his two-volume history, *Virginia's Eastern Shore*, writes that the island was first patented in 1681 by four men: Thomas Hunt, John Floyd, Edmund Bibby, and George Clark. The patent was for 2,200 acres. In 1687 the four received another patent, this time for a total of 3,350 acres. At that time the island was referred to as Hogg Island. The Indian name had been Machipongo, and the island also was known as Shooting Beach. In 1688 the island was divided among the patent holders and their heirs. As was the case with most of the islands at the time, it was used primarily to pasture livestock, and this likely accounts for the name. Feral animals lived on Hog Island into the late 1970s, when The Nature Conservancy had a wild west style cattle roundup and removed the remaining animals. National Geographic filmed the event.

In 1752 Thomas Hunt's heirs sold 139 acres to Peter Dowty, Jr., and Whitelaw speculates that this might have been the first transaction on the island for residential purposes. It also introduces a surname that, with a less phonetic spelling, became widely known on Hog Island. Of the forty-two families listed as Hog Island residents in 1903 by Charles Sterling, eight were Doughtys.

The first people to live permanently on Hog Island were likely there to tend the animals, and the formation of a village probably began soon after the American Revolution ended. The formation of a community on Hog Island had many parallels with the one on Assateague. Both were used as pasture, both had lighthouses and life-saving stations, which employed local people, and both were in close proximity to marketing resources – Chincoteague in the case of Assateague, and Willis Wharf, and later Exmore, in the case of Hog.

One thing Hog had that Assateague lacked was fertile soil, making it possible to sustain a much larger community. Indeed, people lived well on both islands. The sea provided a bounty nearly year around. Migrating shorebirds were killed in spring, waterfowl in winter. The eggs of gulls, rails, and other birds were a special treat during spring nesting season. This natural larder supplemented the vegetables people harvested from their gardens, as well as hogs, chickens, and other animals. Written accounts portray Hog Island as a source of the earth's bounty, where watermelons grew so large they were "too big to steal." Hog Island figs were a cultivar all their own, and specialty nurseries still offer these heirloom varieties.

The people who lived on Hog and Assateague shared similar character traits. Some visitors described them as lazy, but the islanders reasoned that they already had all they wanted and needed, why should they trouble themselves to produce more?

Thompson Holmes wrote that the vast pasture lands of Assateague could support hundreds of horses, cattle, and sheep that could be sold annually, with an expenditure of very little. "The Hebrides of Scotland, so profitable to their proprietors, do not possess the one-hundredth part of the advantages of our Atlantic islands, for all the purposes of comfortable living and extensive stock raising, and yet they are stupidly neglected."

Alexander Hunter, who wrote extensively about the barrier islands for the outdoor periodicals of the day, had a similar attitude when it came to Hog Islanders, and he expressed it without restraint. "Living in a land where no one need work, and where Nature has given them a fine climate, the ocean and land, and food in plenty, we might expect to find as ideal a community as ever existed in Rasselas' Happy Valley; but such is not the fact. The islanders are below mediocrity. There are some bright examples, but the majority are slothful, and their dispositions mean and malicious."

We will hear more from Hunter later.

A more balanced assessment of life on Hog Island is presented by L.E. Doughty in his 57-page memoir published in 2002 by Hickory House. The island offered a life of independence, and it is unlikely anyone went hungry for long, but a life that centered around working on the water was never easy. Doughty writes about oystering, clamming, fishing, and hunting waterfowl, and he does so in a way that makes these activities not necessarily work, but simply a way of living. It was what one did in order to exist.

In that sense, the islanders probably had more in common with Native Americans than with men like Thompson Holmes, who was a doctor, or Alexander Hunter, a government bureaucrat and magazine writer. The natives believed that land and the bounty it produced was like the air. It was not something that could be owned by an individual, but rather an entity that was shared for the mutual benefit of all.

For well-to-do folks like Holmes and Hunter, wild animals and birds were "game," and fishing was a "sport." It was not what one did in order to subsist; it simply provided pleasure, and it was governed by the manners, ethics, and rituals that mimicked those of the countryside back in England. Indeed, John S. Wise, in his 1899 memoir *The End of an Era*, wrote that "In all America, there is no spot more emphatically English than the Kingdom of Accawmacke."

Hunter published an anthology of his hunting and fishing stories in 1908 called *The Huntsman in the South*, and in a story about Hog Island he gives a vivid example of how nature's bounty is perceived. Hunter visited the island to go duck hunting in December 1905 and was staying in the lighthouse keeper's cottage. On the night of December 18, Hunter was sleeping soundly when around midnight someone began pounding on the door. It was Charles Sterling, the keeper of the light, and he wanted Hunter to come at once to the nearby lighthouse. An incredible event was taking place.

A gale had been brewing all day, so Hunter put on his oilskins and left the cottage with Sterling, both men leaning hard into the wind and sleet. They climbed the circular stairway to the keeper's room just beneath the light, and then went out onto a narrow iron balcony, icy with rain and sleet. Thousands of brant, buffeted by the storm, had been attracted to the light. Many crashed into the glass, stunned, some falling lifeless to the ground below.

"The brant, the shyest, wildest, most timid of waterfowl, were within five feet of us, but, evidently blinded by the light, they could see nothing," Hunter wrote. "Some would circle around the tower, others dart by; and wonderful to relate, some would remain stationary in the air, their wings moving so rapidly that they were blurred like a wheel in rapid motion. The lamp in the tower revolved every forty-five seconds, and for a short time every bird was in the vivid glare, which displayed every graceful curve of neck and head, and the set and balance of the body, and enabled one to look into their brilliant eyes."

Soon, many of the one hundred or so people who lived on the island had heard of the event, and they gathered with their dogs in the lighthouse compound, collecting dead brant and dispatching the wounded. Some men wanted access to the lighthouse balcony so they could shoot the brant, but Sterling refused. Sterling himself picked up twenty-eight brant, Hunter wrote, the villagers many times that number.

Hunter was obviously disgusted with the behavior of the villagers, and it illustrates the gulf that had developed between people whose ancestors viewed wildlife as a means of subsistence, and those who view it as sport. To Hunter the event was tragic, and the villagers' actions were savage. But to the villagers it was serendipitous. Christmas was coming and there would be meat on the table for all.

ALEXANDER HUNTER AND CHARLES STERLING

Charles Sterling's booklet, *Hog Island Virginia*, was published in 1903. In 1907 Alexander Hunter published a magazine piece on Hog Island, which included the brant narrative just mentioned. It also included much material from Charles Sterling's booklet, lifted nearly word-for-word. Was Hunter guilty of plagiarism?

About one-half of Hunter's history is verbatim Charles Sterling. The beginning paragraphs are word for word, and much of the other information was apparently lifted directly from Sterling's history without so much as a misplaced comma. But things get interesting when the two writers present the factual information about Hog Island history, and then draw conclusions that are poles apart when discussing the island people. Here is Sterling's idyllic description of life on Hog Island: "The community is as peaceful as the inhabitants of Rasselas' Happy Valley. There is no justice of the peace. No constable, no machinery of the law, for amongst this law-abiding, God-fearing set, there has not been a crime committed within the memory of man."

Hunter's take is that the islanders are too lazy to commit a crime. "There are no criminals among them, for the reason that they have not the energy or spirit to commit a crime, except in the breaking of the game laws. They fish and hunt, and labor for a few weeks gathering oysters, and this labor gives them enough money to live at ease and comfort. Most of these islanders hibernate like an animal; they eat heavily, and then doze for hours. Some of them recline and repose twenty hours out of the twenty-four."

Sterling's 40-page booklet was published in 1903, and Hunter's article was published in *Forest & Stream* in 1907, and it was included in Hunter's anthology, which came out in 1908. So, the dates would indicate that Hunter was the guilty party. But, could there be more to it than that?

In their 1997 anthology, *Seashore Chronicles – Three Centuries of the Virginia Barrier Islands*, Brooks Miles Barnes and Barry R. Truitt published the Hunter/Sterling narrative, and in an end note, in addition to de-bunking the Lost Colony myth, suggested that Hunter might have ghostwritten the Sterling book. Hunter was the published writer, not Sterling, and the "literary style is consistent with Hunter's other work," they pointed out.

This could very well be true. Sterling and Hunter had known each other for years and they occupied common ground. Both were government employees. Hunter worked for the General Land Office in Washington for forty years and Sterling worked for the U.S. Lighthouse Board, first as assistant lightkeeper on Hog, and then from 1901 to 1907 as keeper. They hunted together and when Hunter visited Hog Island, he usually bunked in the keeper's cottage adjacent to the lighthouse. Hunter was not a wealthy railroad executive or New York businessman and was not a member of the private clubs on the barrier islands. When he visited, he either stayed with Sterling on Hog Island or booked a room at the Cobb family hotel farther south.

Hunter was 60 years old in 1903, when Sterling published his book, and it is not difficult to see him playing mentor to a much younger and less experienced writer. As they sat around the woodstove one evening in the keeper's cottage, perhaps Sterling admitted that he would one day like to write a book about the history and people of Hog Island. Perhaps Hunter went to the kitchen cupboard and returned with a writing tablet, a bottle of peach brandy and two glasses, and the men began discussing how best to begin the book.

Begin at the very beginning, Hunter would advise, and go from there. And then Sterling would relate the mysterious story of the colonists who disappeared without leaving a trace. The warlike Indians massacred them, he would say. Maybe it was the mosquitos, Hunter would reply. And so it would go as the evening wore on and the peach brandy lubricated the conversation. The people of Hog Island are so noble and God-like they would never commit a crime, Sterling would exclaim. Hunter would laugh and smack the table with his hand. They are too lazy to commit a crime!

At the end of the evening, Hunter and Sterling would each have a very different version of the same story. Later, Hunter would write a story for *Forest & Stream* magazine and relate the fascinating experience of watching the brant crash into the light during a storm. But for the magazine to publish the story, Hunter first had to include information on Hog Island itself. He needed a sense of place. And then he remembered his evening with Sterling years before, and he realized he already had the story. He had written it himself in the keeper's cottage.

Chapter 10: Broadwater Island

For a period of time, Hog Island was populated by two different groups of people; it had two identities. There were the native Hog Islanders, whose ancestors settled on the island shortly after the American Revolution, and in the late 1880s there came a second group, whose world extended far beyond the Virginia coast. These were northern speculators and sportsmen who bought land and built cottages and a clubhouse on the island in the decade after the railroad opened in 1884. Most were not permanent residents, but they owned much of the land on the island and they gave Hog Island an identity that they created. They even changed the name to Broadwater Island.

Broadwater Island was the creation of Joseph and Elise Ferrell, whose years on Hog Island provide one of the most colorful and far-reaching periods. Joseph L. Ferrell was raised on a farm in Germantown, Pennsylvania, attended Yale briefly, spent a few years travelling, and returned to Philadelphia to start an engineering business. Ferrell married into a prominent family. His wife Elise was from Tennessee and the daughter of Russell Houston, the chief justice of the Tennessee Supreme Court, who later became president of the Louisville and Nashville Railroad. Her mother's side of the family was descended from James K. Polk, the eleventh president of the United States (1845-49).

Elise Houston and Joseph Ferrell met in Louisville when Ferrell went there at Russell Houston's request to design bridges for the railroad. They were married in 1883 and settled in Philadelphia. When Pennsylvania Railroad extended its service southward through the Eastern Shore in the early 1880s, Ferrell worked as a contractor, providing engineering services for the new NYP&N Railroad.

While working on the Eastern Shore, Ferrell discovered the barrier islands and realized that the railroad he was helping to build would make these remote, beautiful islands accessible to millions of city dwellers almost overnight. The railroad opened in 1884, and Joseph and Elise Ferrell went on a buying spree on Hog Island. Between November 25, 1886 and January 4, 1888, they bought three large tracts from William J. Doughty on the south end of the island near the village. They also bought property from Abel Phillips and George Hull, and they purchased more land through estate sales, bringing their holdings to well over 600 acres.

The Ferrells clearly had a plan. In 1890 they formed a corporation called the Broadwater Land and Improvement Company and issued stock at $5.00 a share. They transferred their landholdings to the corporation, with the intention of selling residential and resort

parcels on the island. The Ferrells hired A.T. Mears and Company of Chincoteague to build cottages for their family and for friends and clients from Philadelphia.

Judging from photographs taken during the period, the cottages were rustic cabins made with materials sourced locally. The Ferrells' first cottage was a two-story frame building with single-story additions on two sides. Roofing and siding appear to have been made of cedar shingles. Cedar logs supported the porch roof, and the nubs of the limbs remained on the logs. These made convenient hooks for hanging everything from coats and hats to water buckets. Decorative railing was made from the limbs of trees.

The Ferrells decided to move to the island on a semi-permanent basis to market the property, and they wanted a home with more creature comforts and one that would impress future clients. In 1890 they commissioned the nationally known architect Theophilus P. Chandler of Philadelphia to design a seaside cottage. Chandler, who had studied architecture in Paris, came up with a design that a *Philadelphia Public Ledger* reporter described as "...utterly unlike any other cottage ever built for the shelter of temporary residents by the ocean, or, for that matter, anywhere else. In exterior conformation and interior economy it violates every architectural canon, and is, therefore, both picturesque and comfortable."

Joseph and Elise Ferrell moved to Hog Island with their daughter, Mary-Russell, and began to actively market property. Early on, Ferrell dropped the name "Hog" and replaced it with Broadwater, which had been in use as a generic term describing the vast shallow bays, tidal flats, and saltmarsh that separate the southern islands from the mainland Eastern Shore. Ferrell reasoned that Broadwater Island seemed much more euphonious and marketable than the swine reference, and the name caught on among the news media. The name was also adopted by the post office, no doubt at Ferrell's urging.

A large clubhouse was built in a pine grove adjacent to Ferrell's cottage, and memberships were offered to well-off sportsmen, mainly from Philadelphia. Ferrell was president of the club. In 1904 Ferrell bought a mainland hummock near Brownsville Farm from Capt. Orris A. Browne, and a small clubhouse was constructed where visitors could await transportation to the island. This clubhouse was used as lodging during the latter days of the Broadwater Club.

Ferrell expanded his operation northward, and in February 1892 the Parramore Land and Improvement Company was chartered, with the purpose of constructing residential and resort properties on Parramore Island. The directors of the company were all Broadwater Club members and gave their address as Philadelphia; Ferrell gave his as Broadwater Island, Virginia.

Ferrell also incorporated what likely was the first oyster aquaculture business on Virginia's seaside. The Virginia General Assembly in March 1896 chartered the Broadwater Oyster Association, whose purpose was to "promote, by the application of scientific methods, by experimental research, and by all other appropriate means, the propagation, cultivation, and improvement of the oyster." Directors of the association included three local men – Zoro Willis, O.F. Mears, and G.S. Kendall – and six from Philadelphia.

In November 1892 president-elect Grover Cleveland came to Broadwater for nearly two weeks of duck hunting, and Broadwater Island was in newspapers from coast to coast. Cleveland returned as president the following May for a week of fishing and shorebird shooting, and again Broadwater was in the national media. Ferrell could not have devised a better publicity campaign. News coverage frequently suggested that the entire island was owned by the Broadwater Club, and this suggestion was not quickly refuted.

Joseph and Elise Ferrell's daughter, Mary-Russell, was three when the president visited, and later in her life she recalled sitting in the president's lap when he visited her home, remembering Cleveland as "a nice jolly fat man."

Mary-Russell's Broadwater Island

Mary-Russell spent her childhood summers on Broadwater Island,

and the experience had a profound effect on her life. Ironically, although she spent her childhood as an island girl, as an adult she would make her mark in the American Southwest as a noted artist and a champion of the indigenous art of the Hopis and Navajo of northern Arizona. She and her husband, Dr. Harold Colton, founded the Museum of Northern Arizona in Flagstaff in 1928, which today remains a thriving institution whose mission is to celebrate the beauty and diversity of the Colorado Plateau.

According to *One Woman's West*, a biography of Mary-Russell written in 1997 by Richard and Sherry Mangum, the Ferrell family spent most summers on the island, as well as many holidays. "Broadwater Island had a wide sandy beach, a few meadows, and a pine forest," they wrote. "Mary-Russell came to love it, calling it 'my childhood paradise.' Her hair in bangs and often barefoot, she explored the island on the back of a Chincoteague pony; a black servant named Ben Upshur went along to take care of her."

Mary-Russell was described by the Mangums as a bit of an introvert, preferring to provide her own entertainment. She especially enjoyed fishing, and her parents would tie a rope around her waist and anchor it to a bollard on the Broadwater pier, and she would spend many days safely fishing while they conducted business.

Hog Island had a forested interior, sand dunes, and about eight miles of beach, and Mary-Russell enjoyed exploring, usually accompanied by various animals. "She loved animals," wrote the Mangums, "and in addition to the dogs, had lambs, geese, and chickens; the latter followed her around as though they were domesticated pets."

Mary-Russell's solitary summer days on Broadwater seem to have awakened her need to express herself through visual art. She attended the Pelham School in Philadelphia and was educated there and by various family members at home. Her father taught her mathematics and her mother history, but her favorite subject was art.

"By the end of childhood, Mary-Russell wanted two things out of life," wrote the Mangums. "One was to travel to faraway places. The other was to become an artist."

Unfortunately, the idyllic island life came to an end before Mary-Russell could begin formal art training. "Even though Joseph Ferrell's Broadwater Island project was successful, it did not produce significant income, and increasingly, he concentrated on his first love, inventing," according to the biography.

Ferrell developed a fire-retardant solution that when applied to wood made it virtually fireproof. On May 19, 1903 Ferrell was awarded patent number 728,452 for the solution and the apparatus used to apply it. In recognition of the achievement, Ferrell was awarded a medal from the Franklin Institute of Philadelphia, but his invention did not bring commercial success. During the process of developing the fire-retardant, Ferrell seemed to lose interest in Broadwater and spent less and less time on corporation business. This provoked shareholders, who soon moved to take control of the company and remove Ferrell from his post.

"Joseph Ferrell's finances and health both failed," wrote the Mangums. "According to a family story, a friend and partner in the fire retardant project left, taking the formula with him. The treachery broke Ferrell's heart and led to his death."

Joseph Ferrell died on July 15, 1904, at age sixty-four, when Mary-Russell was fifteen years old. Ferrell no longer controlled the Broadwater Club at the time of his death, but he still owned property on the island, and he remained a principal stockholder of both the Broadwater and Parramore Land and Improvement Companies. In his will, recorded in September 1904 in the Northampton County Clerk of Court, lifetime rights to Ferrell's first cottage went to Miranda Hamlin, and lifetime rights to the "Robbins House" went to Emma Albright. Shares of Broadwater and Parramore stock were left to several relatives, and the remainder of his estate, which included the cottage designed by Chandler, went to his wife, Elise.

According to the Mangums, Elise and Mary-Russell found themselves in dire straits in the months following Joseph Ferrell's death. It became necessary to sell the Broadwater cottage and furniture to cover living expenses, and there was no money to send Mary-Russell to an art academy. A family friend came to their rescue and paid for her tuition at the Philadelphia School of Design for Women. The cottage and furniture were sold to a banker named Schaefer.

Mary-Russell was truly in her element in art school. She graduated in four years and was awarded a post-graduate scholarship for a fifth year. During this year of graduate study, Mary-Russell began to travel, joining groups for extended trips to back country destinations in the American west and British Columbia. On one of these trips, she met Dr. Harold S. Colton, a professor of zoology at the University of Pennsylvania. That would be the first of many trips the two would take, mainly to wilderness areas in the western United States. Mary-Russell and Harold were married in Germantown, Pennsylvania, on May 23, 1912, and left for an extended honeymoon at Valley Ranch near Pecos, New Mexico.

And so, the island girl whose early years were spent riding a Chincoteague pony on the sandy beaches of Hog Island made the transition from east to west, from seaside islands and bays to the high country of the Colorado Plateau. She and Harold would spend their lives in the West, championing the traditional arts of indigenous people, as Mary-Russell found her own way to visually interpret the landscape and the people of northern Arizona.

Mary-Russell Ferrell Colton lived to be 82, and died at The Bells Lodge in Phoenix on July 16, 1971. By the time of her death, Alzheimer's had swept most of the past from her memory. But her biographers say she would sometimes recall pleasant events from her past. "The things she remembered most were childhood days on her 'Paradise,' Broadwater Island," they said.

Paradise Lost

While Joseph and Elise Ferrell created Broadwater Island, the Broadwater Club and all that was associated with it lived on after his death. The Broadwater Land and Improvement Company, whose capital stock sold for $5.00 a share in 1890, was dissolved by the Virginia

Corporation Commission on November 22, 1921, and its assets distributed to shareholders. A $5.00 share was worth $2.05.

The peak years, though, came during the Ferrells' tenure. L. Clarke Davis, a prominent club member and advisor to the president, arranged two extended visits in 1892 and 1893 by Grover Cleveland that put the Broadwater Club in international headlines. In 1894 the University of Pennsylvania football team came for a month of summer practice. They followed with a National Championship that season.

The demise was brought about by a tapestry of misfortunes. A deep recession called the Panic of 1893 greatly affected American industry during the waning years of the 19th century, especially the railroads. While the opening of the railroad on the Eastern Shore in 1884 greatly improved the accessibility of the islands to northern visitors, Hog Island was still separated from the mainland by ten miles of open water. Access involved a trip by railroad, followed by an overland jaunt by wagon, and finally a ride on a steam launch. Other beach resorts were closer to northern cities and were more easily reached. Broadwater was situated to attract the adventurous, not the masses.

And there must have been some dawning realization that islands move. The sea level is rising, the dunes are shifting, the pasture is flooding. One could stand on Hog Island and look southward to grasp the reality. Neighboring Cobbs Island, that venerable and notable resort, was now referred to in the newspapers as a sandbar. The famous Cobb family hotel was lost to the sea in 1896, the remaining furnishings sold at public auction.

The Broadwater Club was dissolved in 1921, although some members still hunted the marshes around the island using the quarters near Brownsville on the mainland. The prime years of the Broadwater Club lasted from around 1890 to 1915, and the village the post office christened Broadwater lasted another two decades.

The Great Storm of '33

In August 1933 a strong hurricane formed in the tropics and made its way north. It came ashore on the Outer Banks of North Carolina and weakened as it moved north. By the time it reached the mouth of the Chesapeake Bay its winds were down to 70 miles-per-hour. Although the storm was a minimal hurricane by the time it hit the Eastern Shore, it caused some of the most devastating floods ever experienced on the coast. Hurricanes were not given names until 1950, but most local residents know all about the storm of '33.

The storm hit the Eastern Shore on August 23, and apparently took many people by surprise. Folks on Hog Island were having a typical day – fishing, clamming, gardening, cooking – when the tide began to rise early that morning. At first, no one paid it any mind, but then the tide kept rising, and people soon realized that it was not going to be high tide until almost noon.

Homes were flooded, and some were washed off their foundation. Animals that roamed freely on the island took to the highest dunes for safety. The coast guard sent boats to rescue stranded people, who were taken to the station for shelter. It was a day that would never be forgotten by the people of Hog Island.

Eighteen people died in the storm in Virginia, including the hunting guide, George Cobb, who drowned near his home on Cobbs Island. Many of the Hog Islanders later told stories of how they took shelter in homes that were floating on the waves.

When the storm ended and the water fell, it was discovered that the tide was the highest ever measured on the seaside Eastern Shore, and it made people realize that, on the coast, the real danger of a hurricane is not just high winds, but what today is called the storm surge. The hurricane of '33 had a storm surge of 9.8-feet above mean low water, and that is what caused death and destruction.

The storm changed Hog Island. It wasn't just that homes were lost and damaged, boats destroyed, livestock lost. Hog Islanders were used to storms – dealing with nor'easters was part of island living – but this was different. Hog Island no longer felt safe.

The Exodus

And so they began to leave, not in a great mass, but one by one, family by family. And they took their houses with them.

The houses were jacked up and logs were placed under them and the houses were rolled onto barges called oyster monitors. It was slow and tedious work, but the men of Hog Island soon became good at it. Houses were moved to locations all over the Eastern Shore, but most went to nearby Willis Wharf. A community east of the harbor today is called Little Hog Island. All of the homes there came from the island.

Most of the homes were moved in the late 1930s, and the storm of '33 is generally given as the cause. But people were leaving before then. L.E. Doughty's family moved to New Jersey around 1923. In his narrative about growing up on Hog Island, he mentions that the Hog Island school had only seven grades. For him to complete high school, his mother moved to the mainland, rented a home, and enrolled him in the Willis Wharf school.

Life on the island had to have been harsh, but the rough spots have been worn smooth by the passage of time. We tend to be sentimental about our past, and no one remains who can tell us exactly what life was like on Hog Island. We have some written records, but these are tales drawn from the clouds of selective memory. No one mentions the mosquitos and green-head flies. There is no envy of cousins on the mainland who have electric lights and indoor plumbing and movies to go to on Saturday nights. No one writes of the child who died of appendicitis because he could not reach a hospital in time.

The people who lived on Hog Island were special. Tough. Resourceful. Resilient. Hard working. They embodied the last of the wilderness spirit. Their lives were firmly attached to the land and the sea. There was a constant awareness among them of the place where they lived. The tides. The seasons. The daily nuances of the natural world. They lacked some of the conveniences of life that we find necessary today, but by another measure they were wealthy people. Perhaps today it is we who envy them. They lived a life of uncluttered simplicity, dependent upon themselves and their neighbors. Their wants were few, and their needs were modest. To revisit them creates a nostalgic suspicion that they lived in a place and time that was like no other.

Chapter 11:
A Presidential Retreat

Most American presidents have had a retreat, a place where they could escape the political currents of Washington and relax with friends and family. Eisenhower had Camp David, Kennedy had the family compound at Hyannis Port, and Reagan headed west to relax at the so-called western white house, Rancho de Cielo.

When Grover Cleveland was president, he retreated to the privacy and solitude of Hog Island. In November 1892, when Cleveland had just been elected to his second term, he spent nearly two weeks on Hog Island relaxing and duck hunting at the Broadwater Club. The president of the club, Joseph Ferrell, was a good friend of Cleveland's, and Ferrell's island cottage became a destination for Cleveland, who was an enthusiastic hunter and fisherman.

Once the railroad opened in 1884, the Eastern Shore became popular among wealthy business people from the north. Gunning clubs were built on barrier islands, and coastal property became a bullish investment. Many of these people knew each other. After the 1892 election Cleveland remarked to his aide, L. Clarke Davis, that he would like to take a holiday to rest and prepare for the coming year. Davis was a member of the Broadwater Club and suggested that the president-elect spend some time on Hog Island, isolated by ten miles of water from reporters and job seekers. When Davis mentioned this to

Joseph Ferrell, Ferrell offered to provide his private cottage as a getaway for the once and future president.

So, Cleveland, Davis, and a few other staff boarded a private rail car in Wilmington on November 23 and arrived in Exmore a few hours later. They then boarded the steam launch *Sunshine* in Willis Wharf, and headed out to Hog Island. The *Philadelphia Public Ledger* on December 1 gave this assessment of Cleveland's first week on Hog Island, which probably was written by Clarke Davis:

> The President-elect is getting at Broadwater Island exactly what he went there to get -- recreation, rest and time and opportunity for consideration of the many grave questions which confront him as he approaches the day when he must again assume the many serious responsibilities of public office, which he probably at no time so much as at present regards as a public trust.
>
> Although Mr. Cleveland is in the truest sense a sportsman, fond of gunning and fishing, with all that that implies, chief of which is a strong, virile, sentient love of nature in all its phases, he did not leave New York solely to secure rest and recreation, to shoot ducks, or to take his ease in the Broadwater Club House, as it was first suggested he should do. He loves tranquility, the association of friends, the free, strong breezes from the ocean and bay, the fine drives and beautiful walks through the woods and on the hard beach of the almost tropical island, and the blue sky above it; he enjoys sitting in the blinds on the broad waters stretching from shore to mainland, and he likes the triumph of bringing down his bird, but his outing means a good deal more than mere personal pleasure.
>
> As he sits in his boat, or in the luxurious cottage which the President of the club placed at Mr. Davis's disposal for the use of Mr. Cleveland and his two friends, he is doing a mighty deal of thinking with regard to the future. That which he probably thinks most of all of is the magnitude of the responsibility his countrymen have placed upon him, confident, assured even, that in highest conscience and to the best of his ability, in the sight of God and man, he will discharge it faithfully according to the strength given him.

Then, as now, the daily activities of the president were highly scrutinized by the news media, and Cleveland's trips to Hog Island were covered in great detail. His post-election trip in 1892 included several days of duck hunting, and it might have been the first time a duck hunt had been covered by the national media. A November 30, 1892 dispatch from the Associated Press described the scene this way:

> Broadwater Inlet rang from shore to shore today with the continuous reports of shotguns, as Grover Cleveland and his fellow sportsmen from the Broadwater Club fired at the enormous flocks of wild duck and brant which wheeled about in surprise and terror, only to be met by renewed volleys of death-dealing shot from another direction.
>
> It was a great day for sport, and the President-elect entered into it with a spirit that showed his appetite for the slaughter had only been whetted by previous disappointments. He was out of bed at daybreak, and was delighted to find that all traces of yesterday's storm had disappeared. After an early breakfast, he left the cottage of his host, Mr. Ferrell, who remained at home, while L. Clarke Davis and Mr. Parvin, of the Broadwater Club, took charge of the expedition, which included four visitors from Philadelphia beside Mr. Cleveland.
>
> The latter was well fortified against the cold north wind, which was dashing the white-caps outside into spray. A pair of high rubber boots reached well above his knees, where they were met by a heavy top-coat of dark gray cloth, buttoned to the chin, with a soft felt hat to match.
>
> Accompanied by a dozen attendants, the gunners were driven to a little cove on the shore of the inlet near the club, where a small fleet of sail boats were moored. These conveyed the party to the blinds, where they could hide unseen by the sharp-eyed and swift-winged water fowl.
>
> Here Mr. Cleveland found another evidence of his host's forethought. Instead of the stationary shelter which he had used last week, a floating blind had been constructed by fastening bushes about the gunwales of a comfortable 16-foot scow, which could be towed to any desirable shooting ground. This furnished accommodation for Mr. Cleveland and Mr. Davis, who were attended by two experienced islanders, George Doughty, a bright young man, loading for the President-elect, and Cut Hargis performing a similar service for his companion.

Cleveland's lengthy stay on a remote barrier island would be unheard of today. He communicated only through daily dispatches that were ferried back and forth by boat to the mainland, and although the media reported extensively on his hunts, media members were required to stay in Exmore, on the mainland, not on the island. Cleveland refused all requests for interviews while on the island, but conversed amiably with local residents.

When the president was not out in the duck blinds, he spent his time reading and visiting with local folks. One of his favorites was Rev. Joseph R. Sturgis, pastor of the church on the island. Rev. Sturgis was described by the islanders as a good all around preacher. "He can preach a good sermon, write an article for the papers, take charge of a surf boat if any unfortunates need assistance, or man a sailboat."

The *Norfolk Landmark* reported that the president's visit dominated daily life on the island.

> Nothing is talked about on the island save Mr. Cleveland, and everything he says or does is treasured up with delight to be retold many times during the long days and nights of Winter and Spring.
>
> "Well," say they, "I never expected to see old Hog Island honored by a President's visit."
>
> His gunning is watched by them, and George Doughty and "Tom," two veteran guides, go so far as to declare that in all their lives they have never seen better shooting than Mr. Cleveland does.
>
> Over on the mainland the people are as ready to praise everything with the Cleveland brand as are the islanders. One party which visited the island a few days brought back a little whiskey from a groggery on the island. It was poor stuff which the groggery retails for 30 cents a pint. It was passed around "as Cleveland whiskey" and those persons who tasted it, many of whom consider themselves good judges of liquor, pronounced it the best they had ever tasted, fully believing that it was really such whiskey as Mr. Cleveland uses.

Mr. Cleveland is Served a Summons

A visit from Northampton County Sheriff Samuel Jarvis created quite a stir on Hog Island during the president's stay. On December 1 Mr. Cleveland and several of his friends spent most of the day in the duck blind hunting brant. The previous day, back in Eastville, Sheriff Jarvis had picked up the mail and found that a summons had been issued for the president-elect by the Court of Chancery in Richmond. On the morning of the first, summons in hand, Sheriff Jarvis went to Willis Wharf and boarded the steamer *Sunshine* for Hog Island. He went to Joseph Ferrell's cottage, where Cleveland was staying, but the president-elect was still out in the marsh in a duck blind. So the sheriff waited until dark for the hunting party to return, and when they did, the news media were with them. The following day, newspapers all over the country published this account by an Associated Press reporter:

> President-elect Grover Cleveland was interviewed last night. The interviewer was not a reporter, but a wide-awake Virginia Sheriff, who called on Mr. Cleveland in his official capacity to serve him with a summons in chancery, brought by James A. Mason and others at Richmond, Va. The official who served the papers on Mr. Cleveland's person was Samuel Jarvis, Sheriff of Northampton county. He learned that Mr. Cleveland was out gunning and awaited his return. Mr. Cleveland returned in the club coach, entirely unprepared for the surprise that awaited him. He entered the cottage with L. Clarke Davis, and was introduced to the Sheriff, with whom he shook hands cordially. Sheriff Jarvis at once handed Mr. Cleveland the papers. The latter glanced at them for a moment and exclaimed, "Well, I've been sued!"
>
> "What!" exclaimed his companion and host in chorus.
>
> "Can you tell me anything about this," asked Mr. Cleveland, turning to the Sheriff.
>
> "I cannot, sir," he replied. "All that I know is that these papers came to me in the mail from Richmond yesterday and it was my duty to serve them."

Mission accomplished, the sheriff left to spend the night with some friends on Hog Island and returned to Eastville the next day. The Northampton Sheriff's Office received a fee of 50 cents for successfully serving the papers.

Cleveland and his party left Hog Island on December 5, but he returned a few months later as president, this time staying about a week. Cleveland came to the island on May 30, 1883 with his aide, L. Clarke Davis. This time the quarry would be fish rather than waterfowl. According to newspaper reports, on the first day the president's party caught about 150 fish, most of which were large bluefish. On the second day rough seas kept the party on land, and instead they spent the morning shooting "snipe, curlews, and other beach birds." By mid-afternoon the winds had dropped off, so the party went fishing, landing ten large black drum among other fish.

The fishing trip of 1893 was the last documented trip the president made to Hog Island during his second term, but Cleveland traveled to the Eastern Shore for hunting and fishing trips after his presidency. He hunted quail on Upshur Neck and stayed at Brownsville Plantation, and he also went on fishing trips out of Wachapreague.

Chapter 12:
Nathan Cobb's Island

On the morning of March 11, 1839 Nathan F. Cobb hitched up his wagon and headed north from his seaside home in Northampton County to Eastville, the county seat. There, as witnessed by the clerk of court, Cobb presented $150 in cash to William and Margaret Fitchett and in return received an unencumbered deed to Great Sand Shoal Island, a sandy barrier beach of some 86 acres lying due east of the village of Oyster.

As the weather warmed in the spring of 1839, Cobb began constructing a modest frame building on the island that would eventually bear his name. Cobb had earlier gotten an ordinary license from the county, giving him permission to serve food and spirits, and he reasoned that the broad sandy beach and the ready abundance of fish and game would entice visitors. Nathan Cobb, who at the time was simply trying to support his family, was unknowingly ushering in what would become the golden age of gunning clubs in coastal Virginia, an era that would reach its summit in the decades following the Civil War, and then slowly fade in the early 20th century because of a rising sea level and the eroding of personal wealth following the Great Depression.

Cobb was a resident of Eastham, Massachusetts, who moved to the Virginia coast in 1837 reportedly because his wife, Nancy, suffered from tuberculosis and doctors advised that a warmer climate might improve her health. They first settled on the mainland near what is now the village of Oyster, and Cobb operated a store and inn prior to purchasing the island. Cobb came from a Cape Cod family of shipbuilders and seafaring men, and it was not long before he decided to leave the retail business and find work closer to the water.

Stories vary as to how Cobb built his hotel on the island. Some say he brought lumber south from New England, others say he dismantled his mainland store and reconstructed it on the island, and still others say that Cobb constructed his island resort from lumber salvaged from ships that went aground on his island. There might be an element of truth to all of these theories. Cobb and his three sons – Nathan, Jr., Warren, and Albert – were in the salvage business; that is, they contracted with ship owners to salvage freight from grounded ships for a percentage of the cargo. This was some 35 years prior to the formation of the U.S. Life-Saving Service, so the Cobbs played an important role in the safety of ships along their part of the coast. The Cobbs were reputed to be tough bargainers when it came to salvaging cargo, but they never sought compensation for saving lives.

The Cobbs' seaside resort was not an overnight success, and the golden age of gunning clubs took some time to gain its luster. The Cobbs made a living by salvaging wrecks and market hunting in the winter, and in summer by entertaining guests and shipping fish and shellfish to northern markets. Cobb apparently paid cash for the island, but he borrowed heavily to add improvements. Most of the loans came from friends and family members, and Cobb was forced to sell parcels on the island to raise funds. He sold seven acres to Elkeny Bracket of Eastham, Massachusetts, in 1840, and he put up the remainder of his land and personal property to secure loans made to him by Henry Doane and Freeman Horton, also of Cape Cod.

According to court records, Cobb's personal property in 1840 included sixteen beds, forty pillows, sixty pillow cases, two cook stoves, six barrels of flour, two cows and one calf, nine hogs, one whale boat with apparatus, and one gun boat with apparatus. All of these were to be turned over to Doane and Horton, along with his remaining acreage on the island, unless his debt was paid. There is no record of the property changing hands, so Cobb apparently settled matters.

"Nathan Cobb was ahead of his time," says Grayson Chesser, a decoy carver and hunting guide on the Eastern Shore. "He had a great idea, and he was a pioneer. He was in a great location, but it was remote and difficult to get to. He was the first and it took a while for the word to get out. When it did, gunning clubs and hotels sprung up on many of the barrier islands."

Chesser says the era of the gunning clubs gained traction shortly after the end of the Civil War. "The country was rebuilding, and industry was booming in the northern cities. This created a class of wealthy business people who had the means and the leisure time to spend on outdoor sports such as fishing and hunting. The Cobbs island resort took advantage of this. They could accommodate something like 200 guests, and they had a bowling alley and all sorts of activities for visitors. They got a lot of coverage in the outdoor press of the day."

Northampton County census records show that in 1850 the household consisted only of family members, with Nathan, Sr. listed as "keeper of house" and Nathan Jr., then 25, as "boatbuilder." Real estate taxes were based on an assessed value of $600. Within ten years, however, the Cobbs' fortunes changed markedly. The 1860 census listed 37 persons on the island, including house servants, hotel keepers, sailors, chamber maids, and fishermen. The real estate assessment was at $12,000, indicating substantial improvements, and by 1870 had gone to $20,000.

The real spark that ignited the boom in gunning clubs was the opening of the railroad on the Eastern Shore in 1884. Prior to that, the islands were difficult to reach, and for most visitors the trip was about the journey, not just the destination. Visitors from the north would take a steamship down the bay to Old Point Comfort in Norfolk, then board a smaller boat for Cherrystone Landing on the Eastern Shore, travel across the peninsula by wagon, and finally take a third boat trip on the seaside out to Cobbs Island.

The railroad changed all that. Travelers could board a morning train in New York or Wilmington, travel south in comfort, get off at Cobbs station, and then take the hotel's launch out to the island where they could enjoy a dinner of freshly caught seafood.

The opening of the railroad saw the development of numerous accommodations on the barrier islands. Some were hotels, like the Cobbs, which advertised for guests in outdoor publications and newspapers, but most were private clubs with a limited membership. Most of the clubs were owned by wealthy businessmen, and most had an association with a northern city.

Private clubs took some business from the Cobbs Island Hotel, but by the late 1880s the old hotel was past its prime. The glory years of the grand old resort began around the end of the Civil War and lasted for about twenty years. Alexander Hunter was a well known writer during that era, and he wrote many magazine stories about the hotel and especially about duck hunting trips. Hunter published an anthology of his stories in 1908 called *The Huntsman in the South*, which has several chapters on the Cobb family and their island resort. Hunter said most of the hotel guests were fashionable people from the city, but they enjoyed the relaxed atmosphere of the island. At dinner, some men would show up in suits and ties, but others would wear the clothes they wore earlier that day in the duck blind. The food was plentiful and fresh, but not fancy. Hunter wrote that if someone ordered fish, the waiter would bring a platter with a trout two feet long, enough to feed a family.

"The Cobbs had little experience in running a hotel, but they knew how to make their guests feel welcome," wrote Hunter. "There was no such thing as social position on the island. Everyone was on equal footing. The Cobbs were so sincere, so true, so democratic that they treated all alike, rich or poor, famous or unknown."

Hunter said that for many years the Cobbs Island Hotel was the most famous resort in America for hunting and fishing. "A week's stay at that place was like taking an ocean trip abroad," he wrote. "It was a fascinating place for the sportsman, and many of us went to the island year after year. The island was a favorite meeting place of the American Yacht Squadron, and in summer all sorts of craft would anchor off the beach, and there would be feast, fun, and frolic."

The Nathan F. Cobb and Sons Salvage Company

Prior to 1870 there were no manned life-saving stations along the coast, and when a ship went aground in a storm the lives of the crew depended upon the actions of volunteers who lived nearby. The situation was similar to the volunteer fire departments many communities have today. Some equipment was provided by the government, but the safety of crew members depended upon volunteers. The shipping industry was growing quickly during this period, and the proliferation of coastal wrecks, especially during winter months, gave rise to a ship salvage industry, where private companies would rescue the crew members of stricken ships, and then contract with the ship owner to salvage the cargo in exchange for a negotiated fee or portion of the goods.

Unfortunately, not all salvage operators were honest. Many stories have circulated about unscrupulous people called wreckers, who at night would use lights to lure passing ships onto the shoals where they would go aground, and the cargo would be stolen by a crew waiting on the beach. In his essays on Cape Cod, Henry David Thoreau wrote disparagingly of wreckers, who would take advantage of a stricken ship to loot whatever goods they could remove.

Some accounts of the time, including those written by Alexander Hunter, referred to the Cobb family as wreckers. The Cobbs, though, were highly respected by people in the maritime industry. The Cobbs saved lives and salvaged ships from the time they moved to the island in 1839 until the U.S. Life-Saving Service opened a station on the island in 1876. And even after the life-saving station was built, the Cobb family continued its salvage business, contracting with shipping companies to salvage cargo or to refloat grounded ships. This continued as a lucrative family business even after the death of Nathan Sr. The Snow Hill *Democratic Messenger* published this account on January 21, 1882:

"Monday morning, January the 9th, a Spanish Barque 800 tons, sailing from Maine and loaded with Iron Ore grounded in twenty feet water at Cobbs Island. The master of the vessel contracted with the Messrs. Cobb for $2500 to relieve the vessel, which they succeeded in doing on Wednesday morning at high water, when the vessel left for Norfolk in an uninjured condition."

The maritime historian Donald G. Shomette writes that "Unlike other wreckers, the Cobbs were generally praised for their humanity and respect for human life." Still, the family built a small fortune over the years, salvaging thirty-seven vessels. Writes Shomette:

> Profit was the main objective for the company, however, and Cobb, ever the shrewd New Englander, never lost sight of it. One of the most important vessels to be salvaged by the company was a coffee bark called *Bar Cricket*, which had become stranded on a shoal quite near the Cobb household while en route from Rio de Janeiro in 1870. The Cobbs efficiently saved the crew and then salvaged both the vessel and its cargo. After a somewhat extended legal contest, Nathan was awarded thirty-five percent of the total value of the ship, $18,000, an exceptionally large sum for the times. Soon afterward, they salvaged the schooner *Henry Lee* and were awarded forty percent of the vessel's value and an incredible sixty percent of its cargo value.

The ships salvaged by the Cobbs carried a wide variety of cargo, ranging from gunpowder to linens to building supplies. Timber was being cut in the forests of the southeastern United States, and ships were sailing regularly from ports such as Charleston, South Carolina, and Brunswick, Georgia, for factories in northern cities. The schooner *Hannibal*, under the command of Capt. William Morse, was heading north with a load of flour from the Haxall Mills in Richmond when it ran aground during a storm. The Cobbs rescued the crew, and most of the flour was saved. No doubt the Cobbs' guests were served many loaves of bread and pancakes in the days that followed.

In the maritime industry, Nathan Sr. was considered a pioneer, a man who set an example the government followed when it established the U.S. Life-Saving Service in 1871. Many of the techniques the life-saving service used in assisting ships in peril were developed by the Nathan F. Cobb and Sons salvage company.

The government had stations on Cobbs Island for many years. The first full time, manned stations in the U.S. were operated by the Life-Saving Service, which was under the Department of the Treasury. Several stations were built on the Virginia barrier islands in the mid-1870s. In 1915 the Life-Saving Service was merged with the Revenue Cutter Service to form the U.S. Coast Guard, which still serves mariners on the Eastern Shore, although, with the exception of Chincoteague, there no longer are active stations on the islands. The Coast Guard station that was on Cobbs Island was moved to the mainland in 1999 and is adjacent to the harbor in Oyster.

The Good Ship Nathan F. Cobb

Nathan died on March 20, 1881, and was buried in a small family cemetery on his island. A few years after his death, a 656-ton, three-masted schooner named the *Nathan F. Cobb* was launched in Rockland, Maine, and soon began shipping freight among east coast ports. In December 1896 the schooner was loaded with lumber when it left port in Brunswick, Georgia, bound for New York. After two days at sea the schooner encountered a northeaster off Frying Pan Shoals, North Carolina. The ship capsized, and then was righted after the crew cut away the masts. The cook and a crewman were washed overboard and drowned, and the remaining crew members took shelter on board, unable to steer the powerless ship. They drifted southward on the northeast wind for four days, the crew subsisting on rainwater and pickled beef, and finally washed ashore on a sandbar off the coast of Ormond Beach, Florida, north of Daytona.

Coincidentally, the *Nathan F. Cobb* wrecked during the same storm season that laid waste to the resort Nathan had built on Cobbs Island more than a half-century earlier. Fittingly, local folks salvaged the remains of the *Nathan F. Cobb* and built a cottage on Ormond Beach with lumber taken from the ship. The wooden ship nameplate *Nathan F. Cobb* was hung over the fireplace. The Cobb Cottage today still stands at 137 Orchard Lane and is part of the Ormond Beach Historic Trail.

Over the years, it became assumed that the ship *Nathan F. Cobb* had been built in honor of Nathan Fosque Cobb, Sr., the man who built one of America's leading resorts and who was a pioneer in the field of marine salvage. If you search the internet for "nathan cobb wreck," you will find numerous references linking Nathan Cobb with the wreck off Ormond Beach.

Wikipedia begins its narrative this way: "The *Nathan F. Cobb* was a three-masted schooner named after the shipbuilder and founder of Cobb's Salvaging Company whose many rescues of stranded ships helped lead to the formation of the United States Life-Saving Service. Despite its namesake's history of shipwreck rescues, the *Nathan F. Cobb* capsized in heavy seas on 1 December 1896 en route from Brunswick, Georgia, to New York with a cargo of timber and cross ties."

Unfortunately, there is no paper trail to substantiate this claim. Who commissioned the construction of the ship? Who paid the substantial price? The Cobb family made a small fortune salvaging ships. Did the family partner with a shipbuilder to honor their patriarch?

In addition, the Cobb family was well known, especially in the maritime industry. Newspapers frequently ran stories about shipwrecks and salvage operations the Cobbs were involved with. If a 656-ton schooner were to be launched in memory of Nathan Cobb, it would be on the front page of the *Peninsula Enterprise*. The *Baltimore Sun* would cover it, as would the *Eastern Shore Herald*, the *Norfolk Gazette*. But there are no news stories.

A British ship registry offers a clue. *Lloyd's Register of Shipping* lists the schooner *Nathan F. Cobb* as having been built around 1890 in Rockland, Maine by the Cobb-Butler Shipbuilding Company and owned by the Cobb-Wright Company, also of Rockland. Was the Cobb associated with the shipbuilding company a relative of Nathan's? The Cobb referenced in *Lloyd's Register* was Francis Cobb, who was born on February 22, 1818 in Cherryfield, Washington, Maine and died on December 2, 1890 at age 72.

If indeed the ship *Nathan F. Cobb* was built to honor the founder and principal of a ship salvage company and pioneer of the life-saving service, there must have been some relationship between Nathan and Francis Cobb. *A History of the Cobb Family*, written in 1923 by Phillip L. Cobb, lists the descendants of Thomas Cobb of Boston, who emigrated from England in the mid-17th century. There is no listing for Nathan Cobb, and although there is one for Francis Elias Cobb, he was born years after the Cobb-Butler Company was formed. There was apparently no familial relationship between the Cobbs of Massachusetts and the Cobbs of Rockland, Maine.

The Cobb-Butler Shipbuilding Co. was begun by Francis Cobb in 1845, and became Cobb-Butler in 1889 when A.W. Butler joined the firm. A history of Rockland says the company specialized in large schooners and was located at the east end of Mechanic Street in Rockland next to the Snow Shipyard. Photographs from the day depict it as a busy, thriving business, with a huge lumber yard supplying material for constructing ships.

There was apparently no familial relationship between Nathan of Cape Cod and Francis of Rockland. But a closer look at the family tree of Francis and Martha Jane Cobb yields a clue as to the naming of the ship. Francis Cobb married Martha Jane Chandler (1820-1895) and together they had eleven children. Of their eleven children, the youngest was a son named Nathan Farwell Cobb, who was born in 1861 and died in 1943. The ship *Nathan F. Cobb*, which foundered in a storm in 1896 and washed ashore on Ormond Beach, Florida, was likely named for the shipbuilder's youngest son, not for Nathan Fosque Cobb, who salvaged ships and built an island resort.

The Last Days

Around 1890 many of the buildings on Cobbs Island were sold to a syndicate from Lynchburg, Virginia, which advertised widely in hunting and fishing magazines to attract visitors who wanted a few days of duck hunting or spring shorebird shooting without having to pay expensive membership dues. The hotel was operated by a succession of local hunting guides. A magazine advertisement in the early 1890s listed T.L. Cobb and J.T. Spady as the proprietors, and rates were $12 per week or $40 per month. Another ad from the same period named C.H. Crumb as the proprietor.

Of all the hunting clubs on the seaside of the Eastern Shore, the Cobb resort was the first to go, just as it had become the first to arrive. It had become apparent that the island was losing land, and a storm in October 1896 did major damage to the buildings. That storm was followed in quick succession by a powerful northeaster, which in early December laid waste to everything the earlier storm had spared.

The *Peninsula Enterprise*, a newspaper published in Accomac, reported in its September 11, 1897, edition: "The sale of the Cobb's Island Hotel furniture took place last week and realized $850. So, the old and popular summer resort is now a thing of the past."

The November 8, 1897, edition of *The Baltimore Sun* reported that the surviving members of the Cobb family had removed the remains of Nathan Cobb, Sr. and other relatives from the small Cobbs Island cemetery and had them moved to high ground on the mainland near Oyster overlooking the island.

The coastal gunning clubs and resorts such as the one on Cobbs Island represent an avenue of Virginia history that is without a footprint. The old gunning clubs are gone, and in many cases the land where they once stood is underwater. Unlike the Civil War, this era has no battlefields to explore, no mansions to tour, no monuments to honor great men and brave deeds. All that remains are a few artifacts, photographs, some written words, and a few memories. And those, also, will too soon be gone.

Cobbs Island today remains as it was before Nathan met with William and Margaret Fitchett in March 1839 and paid them $150 for Great Sand Shoal Island. The island today is owned by The Nature Conservancy and is part of the Virginia Coast Reserve. Great rafts of brant come to the shallow bays in winter to feed on seagrasses, and black ducks settle into ponds that dot the saltmarsh. Watermen catch fish and crabs for market, and clams and oysters thrive in the clean tidal waters that surround the island.

The site where the resort once stood is well out to sea. As sea level has risen in recent years, the island has moved landward, rolling over itself as the beach moves westward, covering what not long ago were the roots of cordgrass. This is the way of barrier islands. Islands move. And when you build upon an island, you must realize that what you put there will be temporary. Nathan Cobb's presence on the island lasted for fifty years, a long time by human measure. But by island measure, it was merely an instant. And not a footprint is left.

Chapter 13: Mockhorn Island

There is a lot of water out in Magothy Bay, but as an old waterman friend once told me, "it's stretched mighty thin." Magothy Bay separates the mainland Eastern Shore from the south end of Mockhorn Island, a 7,000-acre state Wildlife Management Area (WMA) that stretches for several miles along the coast of Northampton County. Magothy Bay is not only shallow, it also includes surprises such as oyster rocks, sandbars, and clam beds which can quickly do expensive damage to boat motors. My son Tom and I were with Conservation Officer Steve Garvis, who has been patrolling these waters for much of his career with the Department of Wildlife Resources, and Steve seemed to know the location of each clam bed and rock. We avoided them all.

We launched at the public boat ramp in the aptly named village of Oyster, headed east, and soon were cruising parallel to a low-lying ribbon of cordgrass that was swaying in the breeze, salt water lapping at its heels. This was Mockhorn -- low, long, and narrow -- an inner island that does not front the Atlantic as barrier islands do, but rather serves as a cushion between the barriers and the mainland.

Mockhorn has been a WMA since 1959, but before that it had a very colorful human history, and on this particular day it was that aspect of Mockhorn we were interested in. At first glance it is an unassuming place, and then you begin to consider its past, and suddenly it becomes much more than a grassy seaside island. Native people hunted and fished here, and there is evidence that Clovis people made birch bark canoes here 13,000 years ago. When European settlers came, this was one of the first places they explored. Captain Samuel Argoll, who was commissioned to fish along the coast to support the Jamestown colony, visited these islands in 1610 and reported "a great store of fish, both shellfish and other." Argall explored Smith Island, just south of Mockhorn, and reported to Sir Thomas Dale, the governor of Virginia, that this low-lying barrier beach could be used to distill salt from sea water. Argall's "a great store of fish" meant little unless this great store could be preserved in brine for a reasonable length of time to sustain the colony over winter. So, salt production was begun on Smith, using large clay vats heated by fire to distill salt from sea water.

Mockhorn soon became a salt producer as well. According to Ralph T. Whitelaw's *Virginia's Eastern Shore*, John Custis, the great-grandfather of Martha Custis Washington, entered into a contract with Peter Reverdly on April 4, 1668 to make salt on the island, which was then owned by Custis. Reverdly was apparently an expert at the salt making process, and a lengthy contract gave him instructions to build 312 clay-lined evaporation ponds for extracting salt from sea water. Unlike on Smith Island, fire was not to be used in the process. Reverdly used solar radiation to distill salt, so it could be said that Mockhorn had America's first solar powered industry.

With Steve Garvis at the controls of the skiff, we cruised the western edge of Mockhorn, looking for more recent evidence of the human past. The northern end of the island is low, with saltmarsh cordgrass (*Spartina alterniflora*) spreading like a saltwater prairie as far as the eye can see. This area of Mockhorn has been a favorite among rail hunters for generations. Lunar tides in the fall drive the water high into the marsh, covering all but the highest stands of grass. These are the few times during the year when clapper rail can be successfully hunted. Otherwise, there is simply too much grass for them to hide in.

As Steve headed south, we saw higher land in the distance -- cedars, wax myrtles, a few scrubby pines. And then we saw two World

War II era watch towers standing side by side on a sandy beach. We were nearing the south end of Mockhorn, and we were closer to finding what we were looking for.

Mockhorn's colorful past includes tales of pirates and Confederate guerilla bands who hid out here during the Civil War. Edward Teach – "Blackbeard" – was supposedly a native of Accomack County, a little to the north, and this was one of his favorite hiding places, so the legend goes. In 1863, during the Civil War, John Yates Beall, a southern espionage agent serving in the Confederate Navy, hid on Mockhorn with his men before the raid that destroyed the Cape Charles Lighthouse on Smith Island and the Union telegraph line at Cherrystone Wharf, on the bay side of the peninsula a few miles away.

But we were looking for evidence of a more permanent nature. In 1852 Nathan Cobb built a hunting lodge here, no doubt to complement the facility he owned on nearby Cobbs Island, a resort that became nationally known from the end of the Civil War until the late 1800s. After Cobb's death the property was purchased by Larimore H. Cushman and his wife Caroline, who by 1902 had purchased the entire upland part of the island in several separate parcels, as well as the vast marshland to the north.

The Cushmans, who made their fortune in the bakery business in New York, added on to Cobb's modest lodge, eventually building one of the last great island retreats on the Virginia coast. The home has not been lived in for decades, but like a ghost, its presence still hovers in a cedar thicket on a bit of high land on the south end of Mockhorn. Steve slowed the skiff to idle speed and nudged the bow onto a sandy beach. Next to us was a row of rotting pilings, all that remained of the dock used by residents and guests when they arrived from the mainland.

We crawled up a bank covered with crumbling concrete and soon were in a shady grove that once sheltered a portico. Some columns still held the weight of the canopy; others were scattered along the ground like fallen soldiers. We walked through the remains of a doorway and entered the large foyer. A stairway on the left would have led to guest quarters on the second story, most of which had caved in. Much of the woodwork, including wainscoting and fireplace mantels, had been removed. A tub remained in a tiled bathroom, no doubt a luxury on a remote island in the early 1900s.

What appeared to have been a courtyard separated two wings of the building. Mrs. Cushman was an enthusiastic gardener, and the remains of some of the plants she introduced were still there. A huge cedar tree had died but was still upright, wrapped by wisteria vines the size of my arm that covered much of the house. The purple flowers were in bloom, and I could hear the hum of bumblebees above me.

We left the courtyard and came to an opening in what appeared to be the working part of the farm. The entire compound was surrounded by a sea wall built of concrete, with local shells embedded in the mix. I realized that this was not just a hunting lodge or a vacation getaway for a wealthy family. A century ago, they lived a self-sustained existence here, something that today might be featured in an issue of Mother Earth News for the well-to-do.

There were many outbuildings made of concrete, a building that appeared to be a smoke house, a dairy, a dozen or so concrete cold frames facing the southern sun, pasture that at one time would have had livestock and chickens, a pond that might have been an aquaculture project. Rusting farm implements were covered with dried brown cordgrass left by the last high tide. The place looked like a medieval fortress of thick concrete, a project that obviously, even a century later, displayed the creativity, the drive, and indeed, the obsession of the owners. I wish I could have known them.

Local historians say the Cushman compound was done in by two factors. The Great Depression of 1929 eroded the family fortune, and the deadly hurricane of 1933 broached the seawall, flooded the property, and covered the fertile land with salt water. Today, after decades of a rising sea level, fields which once grew vegetables and pasture grass grow saltmarsh cordgrass.

After Larimore Cushman's death in 1948, his widow sold the island to Tad Jones, a government contractor from Connecticut who added a modern frame barn, and who often entertained military officials and politicians. Guests would fly in by sea plane or helicopter to spend a few days shooting black ducks in the shallow ponds of Mockhorn and adjacent marshes. The big barn built by Jones was said to be the headquarters of many lavish parties. It still stands today, if missing a few pieces of siding. An amphibious vehicle called "the duck" was used to transport guests to duck blinds some fifty years ago, and it is still there, parked just inside the barn door, a badly rusted old soldier that just might be ready for a final skirmish.

Chapter 14: Smith Island

Smith Island is notable for two things. First, the island had a strong and immediate connection with the Jamestown settlement. Islands farther north in the barrier chain gravitated toward northern cities, but Smith Island luminously reflects the depth and breadth of Virginia history. It was part of the Jamestown colony, and the names that populate its early days are the names we learned when we studied Virginia history in grade school.

Second, in 1970 Smith Island triggered a conservation movement that would shape land use decisions for generations on the Eastern Shore. A New York corporation had bought Smith, Myrtle, and Ship Shoal Islands and announced plans for an upscale resort development with an estimated population of 40,000 to 50,000 people, about three times that of Northampton County. This came as federal and state lawmakers were just beginning to consider how to responsibly use coastal resources while protecting them for future generations.

It is said that America began at Jamestown, and so shall we. Shortly after the Jamestown colony was established in 1607, settlers began exploring the southern portions of the Eastern Shore, including Smith Island. Earlier explorers such as Verrazano and Bartholomew Gilbert probably saw Smith Island while sailing along the coast, but it was not until 1608 that the island was recorded and given a name.

According to Ralph T. Whitelaw's *Virginia's Eastern Shore*, on June

2, 1608 Captain Francis Nelson set sail from Jamestown for England aboard the *Phoenix*, which had arrived in April. As the ship neared the capes, Captain John Smith left it with a party of fourteen men in a small open boat to explore the Chesapeake Bay. Whether the party actually set foot on Smith Island is unknown, but the island was given Smith's name. At that time, Smith Island consisted of a single island about seven miles long. Myrtle and Ship Shoal would be created in the 19th century when storms would cut new inlets through the island, dividing it into three parts.

Sir Samuel Argoll explored the island in June 1613 and found an overwash area where the standing sea water had dried, and when he scooped up a handful, he noticed salt crystals glistening in the sun. "Salt might easily be made there," he wrote, "if there were to be any ponds digged, for that I found Salt kerned (crystalized) where the water had overflowne in certain places."

Smith Island salt brought about the first British settlement on the Eastern Shore. In June 1614, John Pory, Secretary of the Colony, sent Lieutenant Craddock with a detachment of men to boil sea water on Smith Island to make salt, and also to catch fish in the nearby waters for the settlers at Jamestown. The detachment headquarters were on the mainland at a site known as Dale's Gift, which probably was near Old Plantation Creek. Salt was made on the island for several years, and men who had experience in making salt in England and Europe were sent to the island to build ponds for evaporation, which was considered more efficient than boiling water.

During the first decade of the Jamestown settlement, Smith Island, the surrounding waters, and adjacent mainland on the Eastern Shore became vital to the survival of the colony. Great numbers of fish and shellfish were taken to feed the people. When fish were plentiful, they would be preserved in salt for the times when food was scarce. Fertile land on the mainland was used for gardening, adding variety to the larder of the settlement.

Salt making dominated human activity on the island in the early 17th century, and later in the century, as with most of the barrier islands, Smith Island became valuable as pasture land. Smith Island and its 2,600 acres were patented in 1691 by General John Custis, who lived at Arlington Plantation on the bayside west of Smith Island. The Custis family was prominent in Virginia, and nationally, for many years. Martha Dandridge Custis Washington was the wife of President George Washington, and Mary Anne Randolph Custis Lee was the wife of General Robert E. Lee. The Custis family and the Lee heirs owned Smith Island for more than two centuries, and for much of that time used the island as pasturage, raising sheep and cattle.*

George Washington Parke Custis, the step grandson of George Washington, built a mansion on the banks of the Potomac River in 1805 and named it Arlington after the ancestral home in Northampton County. Robert E. Lee and his wife Mary Anne were living at the new Arlington at the outbreak of the Civil War. When Lee sided with the Confederacy, the federal government took over the estate, and it eventually became Arlington National Cemetery.

In 1826 George Washington Parke Custis deeded six acres to the United States government as a site for the first lighthouse, called Cape Charles Light, and thus began a lengthy federal presence on Smith Island. The steel lighthouse on the south end of the island, visible from the north island of the Chesapeake Bay Bridge-Tunnel, is the third-generation light.

The United States Life-Saving Service commissioned its first station in 1875, and George D. Hitchins served as keeper for 33 years (1881-1914), the longest tenure of any keeper on the Eastern Shore. The Smith Island station became one of the busiest of the Virginia islands because of its location at the entrance of the Chesapeake Bay.

Myrtle Island was created in 1851 when a storm cut a new inlet through Smith Island. The 1,000-acre island property was claimed by others, but after lengthy litigation it was restored to the Lee and

---

* For an account of George Washington Parke Custis and Robert E. Lee's experiences at sheep husbandry on Smith Island, see *Seashore Chronicles – Three Centuries of the Virginia Barrier Islands* by Brooks Miles Barnes and Barry R. Truitt, pp. 30-39.

Custis families. In 1857 yet another storm created a third island, which became known as Ship Shoal.

The Custis family and the Lee heirs owned Smith Island for 220 years. It was sold in 1911 to Samuel O. Campbell, a wealthy New York businessman who built a lavish 32-room hunting lodge. Campbell was a bachelor who apparently enjoyed entertaining and was well-liked by his neighbors at the life-saving station. John E. Sterling, who served a tour of duty as a surfman on Smith Island, is quoted in George and Suzanne Hurley's *Shipwrecks and Rescues Along the Barrier Islands of Delaware, Maryland, and Virginia* as saying Campbell "was a very fine man." He said that when Campbell visited the island, he would show up with a wagon load of food and a team of personal chefs who would prepare a fine meal for everyone on the island.

Sterling recalled that on one occasion the station phone rang, and the caller, a brokerage house in New York, left a message for Campbell (who was out hunting) that the stocks he had sold the previous day had netted a profit of a million dollars. Campbell reportedly lost his fortune, and the islands, in the stock market crash of 1929.

From Crash to Conservation

The island was eventually sold at auction and purchased by Richard F. Hall with a winning bid of $40,500. His son, Richard F. Hall, Jr. and his wife, later became owners and sold an option to an Arizona developer who in turn sold it to the Smith Island Development Corporation. The *Eastern Shore News* in December 1970 gave this account:

"According to the two deeds just recorded in the Northampton County Clerk's office, the Nature Conservancy, of Arlington, is purchasing from Smith Island Development Corporation, for $1,250,000 Smith, Myrtle, and Ship Shoal Islands.

"The purchase price includes $561,500 in cash. The remainder bringing the expected total to the $1,250,000 figure is in the form of a mortgage of $688,500 plus interest to be paid over a period of nine years.

"The mortgage is held by Mr. and Mrs. Richard F. Hall, Jr. He is the Accomac attorney whose father earlier had acquired the islands for $40,500 at an auction sale. The younger Hall spent additionally in the islands bringing the total investment to approximately $60,000.

"A big gainer in the transaction was Robert Kailor, Phoenix, Ariz., developer, who optioned the islands from Hall, then sold them to the Smith Island Development Corp., headed by Pierre Lelandais, of New York. Kailor apparently got approximately $200,000 plus annual payments for his promotional efforts.

"The big loser was the Smith Island Development Corp. Including initial costs of $850,000 and various development expenses, the corporation was believed to have tied up about $1.6 million."

The sale of Smith, Myrtle, and Ship Shoal Islands represented a turning point in the way we value salt marshes, freshwater wetlands, and the coastal landscape in general. Books such as Rachael L. Carson's *The Sea Around Us* gave us a look at oceans presented with literary skill and scientific accuracy. A book about salt water marshes titled *Life and Death of the Salt Marsh* by John and Mildred Teal taught us that marshes are among the most productive ecosystems on the planet and are vital to humans in a number of ways. Various levels of government began passing legislation to protect wetlands and water quality. As The *Eastern Shore News* summed it up: "The corporation's plans for a $150 million luxury development on Smith Island ran head on into the ecological crusade which built up tremendous pressures against doing anything to improve the islands.

"Some who had hoped for ready access by local people and tourists to the island beaches were disheartened. Those who hoped for a boost to the local economy and to the Northampton County tax base were disappointed.

"However, those who like to speed out to the islands in their power boats and want the beach area to remain as is, were content. Nature lovers were overjoyed."

Chapter 15: Fisherman Island

Fisherman Island differs from the other Eastern Shore barrier islands in a variety of ways. For one thing, it is a relatively new island. Nautical charts prior to 1815 showed only shallow flats in the area of Fisherman. In 1815 a chart added two small islands called Bird Islands, and in 1853 a U.S. Coast Survey preliminary sketch of Cape Charles and vicinity located Fisherman Island and The Isaacs off the very tip of the peninsula.

The two small islands at that time were separated from the mainland by a vast area of tidal flats, with an average depth of about three feet, and since then those shoals have accreted to become part of what now is a very large island, containing about 2,000 acres of beach, saltmarsh, and maritime dunes. Fisherman Island is growing, and that is something rarely said of barrier islands.

Fisherman Island also is unique in that it is part of the Chesapeake Bay Bridge-Tunnel system. The north-bound and south-bound lanes bisect the island, and it can be said that millions of people visit Fisherman Island each year, but few ever set foot on it.

Like the other islands, Fisherman has enjoyed a colorful past, and although it is a relative newcomer, human history on the island has been fairly constant, and a bit unique. It began not long after the island became large enough to merit a name on a nautical chart.

In the years following the Civil War, American factories were turning out manufactured goods, and farmers were producing food to feed the nation. Consequently, maritime shipping became one of the fastest growing industries in the world. Sailing schooners and steamships were calling in ports from Europe to the Far East, delivering goods made in America, and loading exotic cargos for shipment back home. The world was shrinking, and international trade was becoming an important part of the economies of most nations.

As trade between nations flourished, it created an unintended consequence. Not only were goods moving from country to country, but so were infectious diseases. So, a ship loaded with spices from the West Indies might also have the bacteria that causes cholera traveling as a stowaway in its bilges.

It became necessary to closely monitor ships, especially those visiting foreign ports. The Port of Baltimore had been experiencing incidences of yellow fever spread by crew members and had quarantined suspect ships. In July 1883 a group of medical experts met at Fort Monroe in Hampton to address the problem, and they agreed that it was necessary to screen all ships entering the bay before they headed on to Norfolk, Hampton, Baltimore, or other ports. Dr. G.W. Benson, Maryland's Health Commissioner, told the *Baltimore Sun* on July 31 that the group had selected Fisherman Island as the site for a quarantine station and that operations there would begin immediately.

The hospital ship *Selden* was moored on the south end of the island, and ill sailors were treated there. Two infected ships, the *Californian* and the *Andean*, were moved down from Baltimore and moored on the north end where they were disinfected. Dr. Benson told the *Sun* that the island was perfectly situated at the mouth of the bay in a very remote area and measured about 1,000 yards by 600 yards. There was sufficient water, Dr. Benson said, "to float a navy." Dr. Henry Smith of Norfolk was named officer in charge.

In 1887 Congress appropriated $5,000 to buy five acres on Fisherman, and so began Fisherman Island's role as a national quarantine station. There apparently were a succession of facilities on the island. The first was probably built shortly after the five acres were purchased and likely was built quickly and not well constructed. A news report in the September 28, 1889 *Peninsula Enterprise* said that a strong storm battered the island and damaged the hospital: "the tide rose eight feet and washed away the north end of the island, leaving the hospital in the surf and breaking up the floor. About 200 feet of the island disappeared."

This was the second severe storm to strike the Shore in six months. In early April a spring northeaster pounded the bay and the barrier islands. The *Norfolk Virginian* published this report:

> Capt. Walker, keeper of the quarantine station at Cape Charles, Chesapeake bay, reports to the Marine Hospital Bureau that the schooner *H. Bossman*, Captain W. Boss, of Norfolk, was washed ashore. All hands aboard were saved. An unknown sloop capsized just off of the cape, but owing to the fury of the gale assistance could not be rendered. The damage to the Government hospital [on Fishermans Island] is estimated at $1000. Capt. Walker, who has been in charge of the station for the past five years, says it was the most terrific storm that ever visited Cape Charles.
>
> When the storm came upon a schooner (name and captain unknown) she was driven on Fisherman's Island bar and sunk. The crew and captain managed to reach land in safety, but shortly afterwards the captain died from exposure. The loss of life and shipping property cannot be estimated. Many vessels, it is feared, have been lost on the coast, which will never be heard from. The damage to personal property in Northampton and Accomac counties is estimated at $300,000.

The successive storms of 1889 likely destroyed the original hospital on the island, so the Cape Charles Quarantine Station for a period of time consisted of three ships moored in the area, one for hailing and inspecting vessels, one for disinfection, and a third to serve as the hospital ship.

The station operated under the command of Fort Monroe and was part of the Marine Hospital Service (MHS), which through the National Quarantine Act of 1878 had been given the authority to take over quarantine functions nationally. It served in this capacity for fifty years, and later became part of the National Health Service. The

Marine Hospital Service, like the United States Life-Saving Service, was part of the Treasury Department.

In 1890 the Cape Charles station was one of eight MHS quarantine stations operating in ports around the country. The others were the Delaware Breakwater in Lewes, Delaware; the Gulf at Chandeleur Island, Louisiana; Key West, Florida; Port Townsend, Washington; San Diego and San Francisco, California; and South Atlantic, at the Sapelo Sound in Georgia. Additional stations would be opened as the need arose.

At the Cape Charles station, the *Woodword*, a former ambulance steamer used in New York Harbor, served as the boarding craft. The *Robert Koch* was fitted with a sulfur furnace, pumps, and tanks of germicidal solutions and was used for disinfecting. The *Selden* served as the hospital ship until the permanent facility was built on the island.

The 1891 annual report of the Supervising Surgeon General of the Marine Hospital Service said that from 16 October 1890 to 16 October 1891 the station hailed and inspected 837 vessels. Twelve of them were detained and disinfected. In the following year, 428 vessels were inspected and passed, and nineteen were detained and disinfected. Seventy-three cases of measles and six deaths were reported. The station had eleven officers and crew and an annual budget of $11,597, which was the highest of the eight MHS stations then in operation.

The 1892 season brought about some changes and challenges. An outbreak of cholera erupted in European cities. Cholera is an infectious and often fatal disease that causes severe diarrhea and vomiting and kills by dehydration. It was ordered that all vessels entering the Chesapeake Bay be inspected, and that permits be issued certifying that the crew of the vessel was free from cholera. Without the permit, vessels would not be allowed to dock and offload passengers or cargo.

Construction on the island was delayed because of legal issues over the title to the land, and once these matters were settled, the MHS was faced with a decision of whether to begin construction of a land-based facility, or to continue battling the epidemic using ships moored in the area. The MHS sent Dr. W.H.H. Hutton to the island to assess the situation and he filed this report:

> I have to report that Fisherman Island is quite a large one, probably one-half mile wide and two or three miles long, and lies west and north of the entrance to the Chesapeake Bay. It is partly of rough sand dunes, and partly saltmarsh and swamp. It cannot be approached by vessel except by the so-called North Channel. This channel will carry in its shoalest parts from 18 to 20 feet of water. There is no wharf or means of getting on shore except for wading through surf. There is no potable water on the island. Therefore, until this island is thoroughly equipped with wharves, buildings, hospitals, barracks, and a complete disinfecting plant, it will be in my opinion impracticable to attempt, in the present condition of the island and facilities, to put a large number of persons as suspects thereon. It being impossible, in the present emergency, to prepare this station for the reception of a large number of persons, it is possible to make temporary arrangements for the reception and treatment of a small number of sick on the island, and the well would be vastly better off if held on board the vessel in quarantine until time and disinfection shall have freed them from infection.

The MHS decided that with budget and time restraints, it would be more efficient to quarantine passengers aboard ship. The U.S. Navy training ship *Jamestown*, which had recently been mothballed, was put back into service and fitted as a detention vessel capable of holding 400 to 500 passengers. The revenue cutter, *Ewing*, was secured from the revenue marine service and converted to a hospital ship capable of accommodating thirty patients, with a full corps of officers, nurses, and staff. The quarantine steamer *Charles Foster* would serve as a boarding steamer, and the revenue cutter *Crawford* would carry a marine hospital officer and serve as an additional boarding vessel. The fumigating steamer already in service, the *Robert Koch*, would be used for disinfection.

In 1893 Congress approved an appropriation for construction on the island, and the *Washington News* reported that the project had gone out for bids:

> Bids have been invited for the construction of a pier at Fisherman's Isle, upon which will be placed a steam disinfecting apparatus. A barge is about to be purchased for the transfer of

mail and passengers from vessels which draw too much water, to be anchored directly at the pier. Bids have also been invited for the necessary buildings and tents for a disinfection camp. An artesian well is being bored to secure a full supply of water. With these precautions it is thought Norfolk and Washington will be protected from contagious diseases brought in by steamers anchoring at Cape Charles.

When the cholera epidemic subsided, the Cape Charles station on Fisherman finally got its wharves, buildings, hospital, barracks, and disinfecting plant. Congress approved an appropriation in 1916 for $6,500 for a new boarding launch. And in 1917 Congress approved major renovations to the station, including a new hospital and disinfecting vessel, seven barracks buildings, three mess halls, and officers' quarters. In all, the appropriation was nearly a quarter million dollars.

The Wars

Fisherman Island and neighboring Fort John Custis on the mainland (now Eastern Shore of Virginia National Wildlife Refuge) played an important part in guarding the mouth of the Chesapeake Bay during both World Wars. Eight-inch railway guns were installed in bunkers at Fort Custis during World War II, and the bunkers and a gun are on the refuge walking trail.

On Fisherman, troops were stationed on the island and a number of armaments were installed during both wars, including two six-inch guns and five four-inch guns during World War II.

The quarantine station ceased operation around the time of World War I, when troops were stationed on the island. At that time, there were some fifteen buildings, including barracks, a dining hall, hospital, a weather station, and offices. Most of the buildings were destroyed by fire in the spring of 1922. The *Peninsula Enterprise* reported that a fire broke out on the afternoon of April 16 when a group of people camping on the island built a bonfire which spread to nearby brush. The fire was spotted by an observer at Cape Henry, and a boat with a detachment of soldiers was sent from Fort Monroe, but by the time they reached the island twelve of the fifteen buildings had been destroyed. At the time of the fire, the only resident of the island was a caretaker.

Fisherman Island Today

Today, Fisherman is more important to migrating songbirds and beach nesting birds than it is to national security. It is part of Eastern Shore of Virginia National Wildlife Refuge, and although it is generally closed to the public, tours are offered on Saturday mornings during the winter months, when the beach birds are wintering farther south.

In 1969 the island was declared critical habitat for royal terns and brown pelicans, and it also hosts other beach nesting birds such as piping plovers, common terns, and skimmers. Gulls, rails, willets, and American oystercatchers nest in adjacent marshes. The presence of nesting birds prompted closure of the beach years ago, but more recently refuge officials reasoned that once the birds complete their summer nesting process and the chicks have fledged, why not let the public have a closer look at the landscape they've been zipping across at 55mph in the family sedan.

Saturday morning Fisherman Island tours have become a popular winter outing. Inquiring minds are encouraged to leave the pavement behind and head out into those sandy dunes and onto the beach. Groups of up to twenty-five gather at the refuge visitor center around 8:30 a.m., carpool out to a small parking area on Fisherman, and from there begin a half-day hike that highlights the remarkable human history and natural history of this sandy barrier island.

The tours are led by Virginia Master Naturalists or by USFWS staff and volunteers who are familiar with the history and wildlife of the refuge. My wife and I joined a tour led by George and Jenny Budd, both master naturalists. George is a wildlife photographer and Jenny is a landscape artist. We parked off the busy highway in a grove of wax myrtle trees and began a hike across the island to the beach on the western boundary. It didn't take long to escape the drone of traffic and discover what a remarkably diverse natural system the island supports.

At the very tip of the Eastern Shore peninsula, Fisherman is vital to songbirds during fall migration as the birds rest and refuel before resuming their flight south over the Chesapeake Bay. When we visited, most of the migrants had already passed, but the wax myrtle thickets were full of yellow-rumped warblers, also known as myrtle warblers because of their affinity for the fragrant blue berries of the wax myrtles. Deer and raccoon tracks were numerous along the sandy path, and here and there we found the spent egg casings of terrapins that last summer had climbed the gentle berm of the beach and laid clusters of eggs in the sandy upland.

We peered through a myrtle thicket at a small freshwater pond, where we saw black ducks, widgeon, gadwall, green-winged teal, wood ducks, hooded mergansers, and pied-bill grebes, all on a pond about the size of a football field. In the shrubs behind the pond was a pair of black-crowned night herons. As we hiked through the grass along the pond edge, a woodcock flushed from the undergrowth. "The refuge gets hundreds of woodcock in the winter," said Jenny Budd. "They migrate southward and gather here on the tip of the peninsula before crossing the bay. If we get a prolonged freeze, the birds can suffer because they feed by probing into the soft ground for worms and other prey," said Budd.

A short walk led us to our first encounter with Fisherman's link with human history. Along the side of the trail were tangles of twisted metal, the remains of communication towers used when there was a military presence on the island. Farther along, in a sandy dune, we found the concrete entryway to an old gun emplacement, a relic of World War II era military fortifications.

The concrete bunkers provide the most tangible evidence of military use. Several batteries with gun emplacements were constructed during both world wars, including one with two six-inch guns and two three-inch guns on pedestals. This impressive firepower, coupled with artillery on the mainland, guarded the northern cape during both wars. Following the war years, the armaments were dismantled and the guns sent to army bases around the country. The emplacements where the guns stood were buried.

The military maintained a presence on Fisherman until shortly before the Chesapeake Bay Bridge-Tunnel opened in 1964. Empty barracks, dining facilities, and battery commander and radar towers stood until 1986, when they were demolished by the navy in a training exercise. Today, the only evidence of the military past is in the occasional pile of twisted steel, the remnants of a cross-island roadway, and a concrete pad atop a dune that might once have sheltered soldiers in an underground bunker.

We walked along the wide beach, buffeted by the winter wind, and looked for gifts Fisherman might have left us in the sand. Jingle shells glistened like gold coins in the sea foam. There were razor clams and moon snails, surf clams and whelks and scallops. Now and then we would find the chain-like egg casings of the whelk, or the glossy black, leathery mermaid's purse that once held a hatchling skate. Sometimes there were old fishing lures, a frazzle of monofilament still attached, their once bright colors clouded by sun and salt water. Beyond the breakers, surf scoters drifted in broken rafts on the swells, gulls traded along the shoreline, and in the distance northern gannets soared, paused, and then dove rapidly on baitfish below.

We passed under the two parallel bridges as they left the open water and made landfall on the dunes on the south side of the island. The concrete is massive from this perspective, huge pilings that emerge from the water like giants to support a roadway carrying millions of people bound who-knows-where. We walked under the bridge with heads down, inspecting the wet sand for signs of treasure. Overhead, cars and trucks passed in a white-noise hum, distant and anonymous, like ships in the night. The driver of a tractor trailer spied us down below and sounded a friendly bleat with his air horn. We looked up and waved back, feeling special to be here on this lonely beach, so incredibly remote and yet so well-travelled.

Chapter 16:
The Life-Saving Stations & The Coast Guard

The resumption of international trade by American industries in the years following the Civil War triggered a booming business in shipyards all along the coast. Sail was still considered the most efficient and economical means of commerce, and builders were turning out brigs and barks and schooners as quickly as they could make them. Today we tend to romanticize the age of sail (ships were assigned the feminine pronoun) but the great sailing schooners built in the 1870s and 1880s were designed to move cargo. In today's terms, a schooner would be an 18-wheeler, the tractor-trailer of the sea.

Shipping was a dangerous business in those days. The shipping industry had grown beyond America's ability to provide a safety net, a system of resources to monitor weather and sea conditions, and an ability to react with dispatch when lives and property were at risk. As a result, wrecks were a common occurrence, especially along the sandy shoals of the mid-Atlantic coast, and especially when a ship and crew encountered unanticipated bad weather. Shipwrecks came with a high price tag, both in material costs and in lives lost.

The first attempts to provide a safety network were temporary aid centers on the coast manned by volunteers equipped with some rudimentary equipment provided by the government. These operated in much the same way as volunteer fire departments function in communities today. The problem was that much of the coast was remote, rural, and sparsely populated. A network of bays, marshes, and barrier islands lay between the wrecks and the good Samaritans willing to offer aid.

Unfortunately, the shipping community was seen as an easy target for those with felonious intent. For the unsavory among us, a stricken ship was considered an opportunity, an occasion for plunder and profit. Stories are told of people using lights to lure passing ships onto shoals, where they would be wrecked and robbed. Those who lacked the malicious streak, but nonetheless had an eye for profit, went into the salvage business. When a ship went ashore in a storm, the salvagers would bargain with the owner to save the cargo in exchange for a percentage of the goods.

More common were the recreational wreckers, people who lived in coastal villages who treated a shipwreck as a naturally occurring event, one that inspired not malice, but basic opportunism, a serendipitous chance for an unexpected profit of some sort. The mindset was that when the ship wrecks, the property becomes fair game, the owner's rights relinquished by an act of nature. Finders keepers, losers weepers.

Charles A. Sterling, the keeper of the Hog Island lighthouse who wrote a booklet about the island and its people, described the process this way: "Many vessels were driven by storms on the sand bars, and the people simply helped themselves and paid no salvage.

"There are, in many homes on the Eastern Shore, queer things of a by-gone day, that could tell strange tales: chronometers, huge charts, old fashioned flagons, curious tables and quaint articles of virtu, priceless to the collector of antiques."

As is often the case, it took the federal government some time to establish laws and design a system to close this window of opportunity. Prior to the Civil War, the only life-saving service provided was by a small number of lighthouse keepers who were asked to protect lives with a meager supply of goods and equipment. When war broke out, even that feeble effort disappeared because the government's attention turned to blockades instead of saving lives.

When the war ended, shipping quickly expanded, but the few safety measures that were in place before the war were nearly non-existent, consisting mainly of old, poorly equipped stations between New York and Boston manned by local volunteers. Not surprisingly, newspaper headlines were frequently heralding stories of fatal shipping disasters along the coast. When the public became sufficiently aroused, Congress warmed to the idea of saving the lives of our sailors.

In 1871 Sumner I. Kimball was appointed by President Grant to head the Revenue Marine Bureau of the Treasury Department. Kimball was a lawyer from Maine who went to work for the federal government and quickly made a name for himself. From 1871 to 1878, Kimball fostered the work of the Revenue Cutter Service, which fell under the Revenue Marine Bureau, leading to an increase in the number of life-saving stations along the coast.

In their book *Shipwrecks on the Virginia Coast*, Richard and Julie Pouliot said that Kimball was a master at making the federal bureaucracy work. "Kimball was neither a maritime nor a life-saving expert particularly, but he was an extremely good organizer. He excelled at whatever jobs were given him, and as a result, in 1878 President Hayes appointed him General Superintendent of the newly-formed United States Life-Saving Service. The Senate confirmed his appointment unanimously, without the usual reference to a committee, which was quite a distinction at that time."

Kimball quickly put his penchant for detail to work in developing the chain of command of the new life-saving service. New stations were built, equipment was first rate, and, most importantly, political affiliations were removed from the process of hiring and firing the keepers and crews of the stations. The keeper of the station was appointed by a district superintendent, and the decision was made strictly by the skills, character, and experience of the applicant for the position. The keeper, in turn, hired his own crew, usually six to eight men, who were ranked according to their experience and ability. The crew was made up of members of the community, often watermen who were familiar with the waterways and were skilled at handling a boat in rough seas.

The Life-Saving Stations & The Coast Guard

The keeper was a fulltime employee who worked twelve months a year; the crew worked during the winter storm season, usually from around December 1 until April 31. During the summer months they resumed their work as watermen.

The first stations on the Eastern Shore were commissioned in 1875 and included Assateague Beach, Cedar Island, Hog Island, Cobbs Island, and Smith Island in Virginia, and Green Run Inlet in Maryland. Later, stations were built at Pope's Island near the Maryland line, Parramore Beach, and Wallops Island. The final station in Virginia, Metompkin Island, opened in 1889.

Daily life at the stations consisted of surfboat drills, maintenance of equipment, and practice with beach rescue apparatus. Typical equipment would include a surf cart loaded with a Lyle gun, a breeches buoy, and various lines and pulleys. The Lyle gun was a small cannon capable of firing a projectile to which a light line was attached. The goal was to fire the projectile onto the deck of a stricken ship, have the crew attach the line, and then use that line to retrieve progressively larger ones. Finally, a heavy braided line called a hawser would be attached, pulleys added, and a breeches buoy would be used to transfer crew from the ship to the beach. The breeches buoy was basically a life ring with a very large pair of canvas breeches attached. The crew member would sit in the breeches and the life ring would be attached to a pully on the hawser and be pulled to shore by the life-saving crew.

Under the guidance of Sumner Kimball, the life-saving service established an amazing record. According to Richard and Julie Pouliot, during the first year of operation (1872-73) under his new system, every person imperiled by shipwreck on the coasts of New York and New Jersey was saved. "On these dangerous portions of the Atlantic coast in the winter of 1873-74, some forty-eight vessels were driven ashore. The vessels had a total value of over $2,300,000 but the aggregate loss was less than $460,000. Although there were 1,166 lives imperiled, only two lives were lost. And, both of these deaths were caused by the mast falling when a vessel ran aground."

The stations on the Eastern Shore were involved in many rescues.

Some involved foreign ships, which brought challenges in communication, and some involved local shippers. Captain Polk Lang of Accomac was a well known businessman, oyster grower, and shipper who in March 1888 was rescued by the Smith Island Life-Saving Service when caught in a storm on his way to deliver oysters in Norfolk. The *Peninsula Enterprise* of March 24 had this report:

> Captain Polk Lang, who reached home on Tuesday, reports a narrow escape during the storm of Sunday night of loss of his sloop *Florence Killinger*, together with himself and hand, Jeff Potts. He was lying at Fisherman's Inlet when at midnight she parted cable and drove on Smith's Island. She had lost her rudder and consequently drove at will. Had she missed the Island the gallant Captain would have been helpless at sea in a gale such as rarely visits out coast, and must have been lost. At the earliest possible moment, the Life Saving crew on the Island, under Capt. George Hitchens, reached him, and provided for him as best they could. The crew worked five days on his boat, and finally she was found in sufficient shipshape to sail for Norfolk, which port she reached safely. She was valued at $4,000, and Capt. Lang estimates his loss at about $400. He had bought her only a few months ago and the loss entailed is a heavy one upon him. He is loud in his praises of Captain Hitchens and his crew – each of whom vied with the other in their work and kindness.

The life-saving stations operated on a seasonal basis, which now and then sparked controversy. Early on, the season ran during the winter months, from December 1 through the end of April. This, of course, excluded the hurricane season. Later, stations operated on a ten-month schedule, with the crew being furloughed during June and July.

The keepers of the stations were prominent personalities in the community, and many served lengthy tenures as keeper. During winter storms their business was about saving lives and property, but during the balmy days of spring and summer keepers performed a wide variety of duties. Most were very familiar with the natural history of the barrier islands and were good amateur ornithologists. During the spring and summer bird nesting season, keepers served as wardens, enforcing local laws governing the spring shorebird season. Keepers also conducted censuses of nesting birds and reported these findings to the American Ornithological Society, which published them in its quarterly journal, *The Auk*.

Charles Crumb, keeper of the Cobbs Island Life-Saving Station, was a talented taxidermist whose work was exhibited in natural history museums. Asa Savage, keeper of the Cedar Island Life-Saving Station, arranged a musical program for the Wachapreague Literary Club in the station boathouse. He also managed the annual regatta held each spring by the Accomac Club. John B. Whealton, keeper of the Wallops Island Life-Saving Station, received a commendation and gold medal from the U.S. House of Representatives for his heroism in rescuing the crew of the *Allie B. Chester* during a storm in January 1889. Jack Andrews, keeper of the Cobbs Island Life-Saving Station, was a popular hunting guide.

When writers and newspaper reporters visited the community, the keeper was a good source of information on the human history and natural history of the barrier islands. It was probably one of the few details Sumner Kimball missed when drafting the job description of the keeper, but public relations turned out to be an important part of the job.

In 1915 the United States Life-Saving Service merged with the Revenue Cutter Service to form the United States Coast Guard. The coast guard had a presence on the barrier islands for another forty years, and as methods of travel and communication changed in the 1950s, stations began to close, consolidate, or move to the mainland. The life-saving station on the south end of Metompkin Island was damaged by the storm of 1933 and was replaced by the Metompkin Inlet Coast Guard station built on the north end of Cedar. It was deactivated in the 1950s, but it still stands, owned by a group of families who use it as a vacation lodge. The last station to close was Parramore Beach, which was built on the north end of the island in 1937. The station was deactivated on September 15, 1994 and was destroyed by fire on April 4, 1999 after being struck by lightning. The station was owned by The Nature Conservancy and was being converted to educational use at the time of the fire.

Fire has destroyed many of the government structures on the islands, including both the life-saving station and coast guard station on the north end of Parramore, two generations of coast guard stations on the north end of Hog Island, the coast guard station on the south end of Hog, the original life-saving station on the south end of Cobbs (It burned suspiciously before it was activated.), the lighthouse keeper's dwelling on Smith, and the hospital and quarantine station on Fisherman. The coast guard station on the south end of Cobbs was moved to a mainland site near Oyster in 1999.

Parramore and the Tale of Two Esks

In the fall of 1888, during a period of less than a week, two ships wrecked off the beach at Parramore Island. In an uncanny coincidence, both were named the *Esk*. To add mystery to the coincidence, one of the *Esks* reappeared as a ghost ship twelve years later.

The first *Esk* to go down was built in 1885 and named for a wealthy Scots-Canadian lumber merchant named Robert Montague Esk. The three-masted schooner was built in Maine and did duty hauling railroad cross ties for the Baltimore and Ohio Railroad early in life. After being damaged in a storm in 1887 off Smith Island she was re-fitted and went back to work hauling guano from the Caribbean Islands to ports in Norfolk and Baltimore. Guano, used to make fertilizer, consisted of the waste of birds and bats and was collected wherever there were nesting colonies. As droppings built up over time, they would be scraped up, packaged, and shipped to fertilizer factories. Crews, consisting mainly of black men, were being shipped out of coastal cities such as Baltimore and Norfolk to work on guano islands in the Caribbean.

The *Esk* made three voyages to the guano islands in the summer of 1888, and on her last trip sailed from Sombrero Island with a full cargo and thirty-two laborers, due to arrive in Norfolk on September 9. A hurricane swept up the coast on September 7 and 8, and the *Esk* failed to arrive in Norfolk on time. On September 30 she was reported overdue, and later described as missing. Finally, by 1890, she was declared as "lost with all aboard."

The second *Esk* was a British ship and was probably named for the River Esk, which flows through Yorkshire, England and empties into the North Sea. She was bound from Maracaibo, South America, to Providence, Rhode Island, with a cargo of 180 tons of dyewood, valued at $3,500, when she wrecked on Parramore Beach during a gale. The *Peninsula Enterprise* reported in its September 15, 1888 edition that "the captain, W. F. Watt, and the entire crew, all of Nova Scotia, were rescued by the crew of the life-saving station in charge of Capt. N. B. Rich, at imminent peril to their own lives. The cargo was also saved, and is now in the hands of the underwriters." The vessel was battered by the surf and was a total wreck.

For twelve years nothing was found of the first *Esk*, no wreckage, no bodies, nothing that would provide a clue as to what happened to the ship. But in the winter of 1900, a northeaster pounded the coast for several days. The stormed rolled over the barrier islands, closing inlets here and opening them there. At the height of the fury a deep gut was cut into the beach off Parramore Island, and finally on the third day the storm subsided and the seas lay calm.

As the clouds parted, a three-masted schooner was spotted 200 yards offshore, directly in front of the U.S. Life-Saving Station. The station keepers boarded her and found a badly damaged ship that obviously had been at the mercy of the sea for a long time, covered with growth, her deck attacked by worms. There was no evidence of human remains on board, although the crew was able to salvage her wheel, compass, lanterns, and the master's sextant. But her name board survived, and cut deep into the pine plank was the name *Esk*.

The remains of the *Esk* lay on the beach on Parramore for years, often photographed by visitors and picked over by souvenir seekers. The mystery, though, was to which *Esk* did the remains belong? The answer is most likely the first *Esk*, the one in which thirty-two workers and the crew tragically died. The second *Esk* was battered to pieces by the sea, according to newspaper reports. The first *Esk* went down in deeper water, and there she lay for a dozen years until being awakened by a northeaster.

The Wreck of the San Albano

The majority of the rescues performed by the life-saving service on the Eastern Shore involved ships traveling the coastal routes between New York or Boston and southern ports such as Savannah and Charleston. Many of the rescues were reported in local newspapers, especially when they involved crews and ships from nearby ports. But in 1892 the men of the station at Hog Island rescued a steamship from Spain, saving a crew of twenty-six Spanish sailors, and their act of bravery made world news. Later that year, the king of Spain ordered that the keeper and crew be presented medals of honor recognizing their heroism.

The incident began early on the morning of February 23 when surfman J.R. Dunton was patrolling the beach during a northeast storm. The surf was crashing high on the berm of the beach and sending sea foam to the dune line. The rain was swirling in the wind, mixing with the froth stirred up by the surf, and through the wet darkness, Dunton thought he saw lights. He leaned into the wind and listened, but he could hear nothing but the pounding surf. But then, through the darkness, he saw them again. They were the running lights of a ship, and they were close to the shore. Much too close to the shore.

Dunton quickly reached into his pack for a Coston flare, lighted it, and held it aloft, waving it in an attempt to get the captain's attention, warning him that his ship was in danger. In less than a minute, the lights disappeared, but Dunton didn't know whether the captain had seen the flare and steered seaward, or if the ship had simply slipped into the darkness once again.

Dunton hurried back to the station and reported what he had

seen to keeper John E. Johnson, who went to the lookout tower with his field glasses. At first, Johnson could see nothing, but as dawn approached, the skies slowly went from black to gray, and through the glasses Johnson could make out the masts of the ship over the rims of the sand dunes. He sounded the alarm.

The vessel was a 1,291-ton Spanish steamship built in 1880 called the *San Albano*, sailing out of the port of Bilbao, Spain, heading from New Orleans to Hamburg with a load of cotton, grain, and oil. Laden with cargo, the *San Albano* was drawing nearly 21 feet of water, and she was way too close to shore. The vessel grazed an offshore sandbar, bounced off with the next swell, and when she settled into a trough the captain set his anchors.

The ship was badly off course. The captain's intent was to stop at the port of Hampton Roads to load coal before making the ocean crossing, but the storm made the identification of landmarks difficult, and the captain had passed by Cape Henry and Cape Charles without seeing the lights. The ship came to rest about six miles north of the Hog Island life-saving station, about 500 yards offshore. As the waves came they would lift the ship, and when they retreated she would pound the bottom. Over and over again.

Finally, the *San Albano's* hull gave way and she settled into the trough, the seas breaking over her. Re-floating the vessel was now out of the question; the task now would be to safely remove the crew before the ship broke up. The men of the life-saving service go through endless drills in the station yard, and they keep their equipment in immaculate condition. On the morning of February 23, 1892, they learned the value of those boring drills and endless preparation.

Keeper Johnson ordered the apparatus cart brought to the scene. The cart carried a Lyle gun, powder charges, lines of various sizes, and first aid gear. He also ordered the surf boat and life car, and thus had options. If the Lyle gun failed to secure a lifeline, the men would attempt to reach the ship by boat, an option, but not a pleasant one. It took several hours for the equipment to be moved through sand and water from the station to the site of the grounding, and it was late afternoon by the time the Lyle gun was set up.

The purpose of the gun was to launch a light line to the deck of the stricken ship, have the crew secure it, and then use that line to convey heavier ones. Finally, a breeches buoy would be attached and used to remove the crew one-by-one to safety. The first shot from the Lyle gun fell short, but the second landed on the deck. The Spanish crew, unable to read the instructions for securing the line, did not fasten it properly and when the crew on the beach tightened it, the line gave way. More launches from the Lyle gun fell short, and the rising tide was increasing the range needed to reach the ship.

Meanwhile, seven members of the *San Albano* crew launched the only lifeboat remaining on the ship and miraculously made it to shore. One man went missing when he attempted to swim to shore with the aid of a wooden plank. The good news was that the crew on shore reported that the wreck was still solid and the deck houses were dry.

Keeper Johnson decided to have his men return to the station for food and rest and left a crew of volunteers organized by Reverend J.R. Sturgis to maintain a bonfire on the beach. A horse was left in case the situation changed and the keeper needed to be notified quickly.

After resting for a few hours, the crew returned to find the situation virtually unchanged. The tide was lower, but the *San Albano* was still beyond the range of the Lyle gun. Keeper Johnson had an idea. The Lyle gun is typically fired from the beach, but if it were loaded into the apparatus cart and pushed into the breakers, the range would be reduced. The men attached the gun to the deck of the cart and pushed it through the surf to waist-deep water. The first shot cleared the rail and the Spanish crew this time secured the line properly, and within an hour the life cart was removing the remaining nineteen crew members one by one. Of the crew of twenty-seven men, all were saved except one, who had the poor judgement to swim to shore. The men also saved the ship's cat.

The Spanish sailors were taken to the life-saving station where they were fed and given clothes donated by the Women's National Relief Association. They remained at the station for a week, until transportation to the mainland could be arranged. The *San Albano* broke up in the surf of Hog Island, its cargo of cotton, grain, and oil, valued at $120,000, a total loss.

The rescue of the *San Albano* was one of the most notable of the year for the United States Life-Saving Service. The inspector who investigated the incident filed this report: "Great credit is due the keeper and the crew of the Hog Island Station for their brave and persistent efforts, and every man did his whole duty. The people of the island were prompt and ready to assist the life-saving crew in every way possible."

A few months later, the government of Spain honored the life-saving crew, and the king of Spain ordered that medals be made to honor the keeper and each crew member. Those receiving medals and commendations were John E. Johnson, keeper of the station, and surfmen R.C. Joynes, J.R. Dunton, C.F. Carpenter, J.H. DeWald, J.E. Smith, J.K. Carpenter, J.A. Doughty, and William B. Goffigon.

In November of that year, President-elect Grover Cleveland visited Hog Island for a duck hunting trip, and while there he personally congratulated the members of the life-saving service. It was Reverend Sturgis, apparently, who told him of the crew's heroic act.

Chapter 17:
Peninsulas in Repose
The Necks of the Eastern Shore

I have a friend in Oregon who collects words. Specifically, she collects words that are old and seldom used anymore but still manage to evoke an image that is unique and thought provoking. When she finds such a word, she shares it with family and friends. Her word-gift recently was "demi-isle," a word that was used to describe a peninsula before peninsula became part of the English language.

She knows that we live on a peninsula, or demi-isle, and I told her that our large peninsula is actually made up of many small peninsulas, which we call "necks." Delmarva is obviously and emphatically a peninsula, with the Atlantic on one side and the Chesapeake on the other, but within the bounds of Delmarva are dozens of tracts of land that meet the definition of peninsula. That is, a narrow strip of land surrounded on two or three sides by water. And, unlike the Delmarva peninsula, most necks are not arranged vertically, north and south, but horizontally, like peninsulas in repose.

Eastern Shore necks are a complement to our seaside islands and bayside beaches and marsh meadows. The English settled in wooded areas along the coast that were accessed by navigable creeks and streams, and as the population grew, wooded necks became the places where people chose to live. Necks became the original American community. The "neck of the woods" was your home.

"Any bears where you live?"

Peninsulas In Repose: The Necks of the Eastern Shore

"Never seen one in our neck of the woods."

In the early years, people settled in the wooded necks where land was fertile and dry. Sheep, cattle, and horses were pastured on the barrier islands and bayside marshes, and animals adjusted to a natural diet of spartina grasses, shrubs, and vines such as greenbrier. As long as fresh water was available, the animals did fine. Pasturing animals on islands saved greatly on feed costs, and it kept them out of fields where planters were attempting to grow corn, tobacco, and other crops.

Towns are a comparatively modern concept on the Eastern Shore, many a product of the railroad, which began rolling in 1884. Necks don't show up on state highway maps or county road maps, although road signs still let you know you're travelling on Upshur Neck Road, or perhaps Arbuckle Neck Road. Google Earth does identify many necks, but the best way to vicariously explore our necks is to get out the venerable and reliable U.S. Geological Survey topo maps. Most are based on aerial photographs taken more than 50 years ago, but necks are reasonably stable landforms that rarely move great distances.

No one seems to know the origin of the term "neck," but it has been around for a long time. The easy assumption is that it was imported by the English when they colonized the region in the early 1600s, but my friends Terry and Judy Malarkey, who are from England, say they had never heard of the term until moving to the Eastern Shore. One theory is that the English purposely assigned new names to landforms in the new world. Rather than using traditional English terms such as heath, moor, fen, and dell, they came up with hollow, gap, branch, neck, and gut – new, uniquely American names.

The Eastern Shore has some forty named necks on the seaside and bayside, beginning on the south with Old Plantation Neck, which is bordered by Old Plantation and King's Creek. Farther north are Eyre Hall and Eyreville Neck, and Savage Neck in Northampton County. The northernmost neck is Winders Neck in upper Accomack, which is defined by the waters of Swans Gut Creek, Coldkill Creek, and Chincoteague Bay.

As noted earlier, most of our necks are peninsulas in repose, created by creeks that run perpendicular to the spine of the Eastern Shore. Two notable exceptions are Upshur Neck and Bells Neck, which are parallel to each other, and separated by Hog Island Bay, Machipongo River, and Parting Creek, from east to west.

The Franktown area on the bayside is threaded by numerous waterways and thus has many necks, including, from north to south, Occohannock, Wellington, Elliotts, Church, Wilsonia, Old Town, and Great Neck. The necks are formed by the Nassawadox, Church, Hungars, Jacobus, Savage, and Mattawoman Creeks and their tributaries.

The Shore's link with space exploration, NASA's Wallops Flight Facility, is located on Wallops Neck, a product of waterways that include Mosquito Creek, Little Mosquito Creek, Simoneaston Bay, and Simoneaston Creek.

But long before the name Wallops became synonymous with space flight, the area was known as the home of the Wallops Neck goosery. The goosery was a farm where the Industry Down and Quilting Company of Philadelphia raised white geese, whose feathers and down would be slept upon by thousands of Americans in the 1880s. The goosery was a boon for local grain farmers, who provided corn for the flock of geese. In 1884 the *Peninsula Enterprise* reported that the company had recently spent $1,000 among local farmers, and still was looking for more corn. "Some of our people think that if this thing continues, corn bread will be scarce," quipped a writer for the newspaper.

The goosery began operation in May 1883 when the Philadelphia corporation bought a farm in Wallops Neck from C.T. Taylor, who lived west of Wallops in Jollys Neck, which is bordered by Holden and Bullbeggar Creeks. According to the *Peninsula Enterprise*, the corporation paid $5,000 for the land, making Mr. Taylor a wealthy man. The corporation constructed quarters to house 1,900 geese on the farm.

Most of the necks on the Shore reflect the names of the original patent holders of land, or those of families who had substantial acreage. These include families who were prominent in Eastern Shore history, with names such as Savage, Custis, Upshur, Scarburgh, Wallop,

White, Joynes, Bayly, Bell, Brickhouse, Parker, Arbuckle, and Hack. Many of the necks are created by waterways with names reflecting the Native American presence, but most of the necks are named for English settlers.

The necks more closely resemble ribs than they do necks. If the backbone of the Eastern Shore is its spine, running more or less north and south, then the necks are ribs. stretching from the open water of the Chesapeake Bay and the Broadwater of the seaside inland toward the spine. In the years before the railroad drew people to the spine of the Shore, the area was densely wooded. We had necks of the woods on the seaside and bayside, separated by navigable waterways. The forested area that ran along the spine of the Eastern Shore was referred to as the mid-woods, according to historian Brooks Miles Barnes.

Necks were the original communities of the Eastern Shore, easily accessible by water to facilitate trade and travel, populated by people with a common bond; they lived and worked in the same neck of land. Early colonists chose as homesites wooded land that was near navigable water. The Native Americans preferred land that had fertile soil, fresh water for drinking and cooking, and they valued freshwater or brackish wetlands rather than deep water for navigation. In those wetlands grew grasses and reeds the people used for making tools and baskets, and in the swamps they found emergent plants such as arum, whose roots were used in cooking.

Perhaps the most storied of the Eastern Shore necks is Savage Neck, named for Thomas Savage, said to have been the first Englishman to settle permanently on the peninsula. Thomas arrived in Jamestown on January 2, 1608 in the ship *John and Francis*, whose captain was Christopher Newport. Thomas was 13 at the time. Captain John Smith later wrote that Thomas was given to Debdeavon, the Laughing King, and lived among the native people for a number of years. Thomas became fluent in the native languages and often served as an interpreter in dealings involving the colonists and native people.

Thomas was given a large tract of land in payment for his services in establishing trade. The land includes what is now Savage Neck and the county seat, Eastville. The neck is bordered on the north by The Gulf, or Savage Creek, which once provided access by water to the county court and other government offices, and on the west by Chesapeake Bay. On the south is Cherrystone Inlet and Cherrystone Creek. Eastville (once known as The Horns) is the head of Savage Neck, and was the seat of government for Northampton County and was thus a busy community. Savage Neck is perhaps best known today for the towering sand dunes along the beach south of the Smith's Beach community. The dunes, the maritime forest, and a mile of shoreline are protected by the state as the Savage Neck Dunes Natural Area Preserve.

Necks are communities defined by natural boundaries, not political ones. It is often difficult to say exactly where a neck begins, but it's certain as to where it ends. When your feet get wet, you've reached the boundary. Necks have no geo-political infrastructure. There is no mayor and council and most are not named on maps. What they do have is a colorful history; some were home to early political leaders and influential people within the colony. Others had a dark side. Sluitkill Neck, near Cashville, was the scene of a grisly murder in 1885.

Living on a neck in the early days of settlement was not unlike living on an island. Isolation brought people closer together through both social and familial bonds. Typically, a neck would be populated by families that had large landholdings, but gradually, as more people moved onto the land and as families expanded, the population became more diverse. Early settlers did not follow the tradition of primogeniture, in which land is left to the eldest son, so large families meant that family land could be divided numerous times over the generations. In addition, life expectancy was comparatively short, so land was often transferred during re-marriages.

Although the necks were isolated from the mainland, there was a great sense of community within the neck itself. James R. Perry, in his book *The Formation of a Society on Virginia's Eastern Shore, 1615-1655*, writes that social cohesion was very strong, with people providing for both family members and neighbors. "People turned to their neighbors for an exchange of sociability and favors as well as responsibilities," he wrote. "Individually and collectively, neighbors also exercised a degree of social control. This skein of interactions helped to bind landowners together on the Eastern Shore."

The necks along the seaside and bayside offered everything settlers needed, so there was little interest in moving to the central spine, the mid-woods. The water provided food and a means of travel, and a social network provided contact with family and friends and security.

"A century and a half ago (circa 1800) the Virginia Eastern Shore's communities were almost entirely on or not far from the bayside creeks or the seaside inlets," wrote James Egbert Mears in the 1950 anthology *The Eastern Shore – Maryland and Virginia*. "There were few villages in the center of the peninsula until after 1884, with the completion of the New York, Philadelphia and Norfolk Railroad; in fact, when it began operating it passed through not a single village between New Church and the new town of Cape Charles."

Necks are a geological phenomenon, the serendipitous placement of high land near deep water. The great majority of Eastern Shore necks are on the bayside of Northampton County and the seaside of Accomack. Northampton's seaside is noted for its vast Broadwater, miles of shallow water, marshy islands, tidal flats, and meandering channels. When a blue-eyed British dandy explored the area looking for a place to settle, the high banks of Nassawadox Creek had vastly more appeal than a seaside mud flat.

The converse is true in Accomack. The northern county's bayside is a maze of tidal creeks threading vast spartina marshes, interrupted now and then by marginal high lands called hammocks, or hummocks, most of them an acre or two of stunted pine, cedar, holly, wax myrtle, and groundsel. It's a beautiful landscape, but not given to growing corn and tobacco.

Accomack's necks are clustered along the seaside, where the barrier islands hug the mainland and tidal creeks meander into fertile, sandy soil. Folly Creek was the avenue by which most residents reached the county seat, then known as Drummondtown. Ten named necks lie on the seaside from Accomac north, and most of them recognize prominent landowners and leaders. The names could be taken from the index of a book on Eastern Shore history. There is Custis, Joynes, Bayly, Parker, White, Arbuckle, Wallops, and Winder. They are joined by Gargathy, which is derived from Gargaphia, the name of a colonial era plantation, and Hog, which reflects the ancient practice of pasturing animals on the islands and marshes. In Accomack, we have Hog Island, Hog Neck, Hog Creek, and Hog Neck Creek.

Although Accomack has Pitt's Neck and Jollys Neck near the northern boundary, most of the necks on the bayside begin south of the marshlands of Saxis, Cattail Neck, and Parkers Marsh. An exception would be Coe's Out Neck, an area between Muddy Creek and Guilford Creek settled by Timothy Coe around 1660. The tract is mostly marshland, but Coe built a plantation on the high land and supposedly had a lumber mill on the property. The head of Coe's Out Neck would have been the community of Guilford, one of the oldest settlements in Accomack County. Another exception would be Pocomoke Neck, which lies between Holden and Messongo Creeks. It was also referred to as Freeschool Neck and Messongo Neck.

The majority of the bayside necks begin on the south shore of Onancock Creek with Baileys Neck, Finneys Neck (There also is Finneys Creek and Finneys Island.), Broadway Neck, and Sluitkill Neck. Sluitkill implies perhaps a Dutch influence ("kill" meaning small creek in Dutch.), But spellings in various old publications and records vary greatly, including Sluthkill, Slutkiln, Slutkill, and various others.

South of Onancock Creek, the bayside necks are relatively well-defined. Yeo Neck, home of the Eastern Shore Yacht and Country Club, is formed by Pungoteague and Taylor Creeks. Between Pungoteague Creek and Nandua Creek lies Hacks Neck, which is probably the only Eastern Shore neck to have a book published about it. *Hacks Neck and Its People, Past and Present*, a history and genealogy of the George Hack family and their associates, was published in 1937 by James Egbert Mears. Pungoteague was the head of Hacks Neck, with the requisite churches, inns, bars, stores, and other improvements.

Peninsulas In Repose: The Necks of the Eastern Shore

If you take Rt. 178 from Pungoteague south to Craddockville, you will skirt the eastern boundaries of Fairview Neck, Island Neck, Craddock Neck and Scarburgh Neck. Craddock Neck lies between Nandua Creek and Craddock Creek and consists mainly of farmland and woodland. If you keep straight on Rt. 615 instead bearing left on Rt. 178, you will soon be in Scarburgh Neck. The road comes to an uncelebrated end at a boatyard in Davis Wharf, one of the ancient landings on Occohannock Creek. Look across the creek and you will see Morley's Wharf (formerly Read's Wharf), an equally ancient landing serving the residents of Occohannock Neck in Northampton County. Davis Wharf and Morley's Wharf served the farming communities of Scarburgh Neck and Occohannock Neck from the early days of settlement until the railroad and motor truck gradually supplanted sail and steamboats as the preferred method of getting farm produce to markets and city goods to rural homes.

Scarburgh Neck is larger than Craddock Neck, and Occohannock is larger than both. Occohannock Creek flows deeply into the Eastern Shore peninsula, separating the two counties. Its upper branches (Taylor Branch is the largest.) reach almost to Rt. 13 and north to the pond at the Agricultural Experiment Station near Painter. Occohannock Neck is a mixture of agriculture and residential use, and is known by generations of Eastern Shore residents for its beaches. Silver Beach has been a popular summer community for years and a gathering spot for young people from both counties.

Unlike most of the necks farther north, Occohannock has a great deal of high, fertile land, making it one of the leading farming communities on the Eastern Shore. The neck is bordered on the north by Occohannock Creek, on the west by Chesapeake Bay, and on the south by Nassawadox Creek. The prominent shoreline, fertile soil, and the nearness of deep water made it a favorite of early settlers. Drive through the farm fields and glance at the meandering waters of Nassawadox Creek far below, and the appeal of the landscape is obvious.

When the railroad opened on the Eastern Shore in 1884 the great productivity of Occohannock Neck farms made a compelling case for extending a 12-mile spur line from Exmore through the communities of Wardtown and Jamesville to mine the wealth of truck crops grown in the region. But the rail spur never materialized, and farmers continued to send crops to market by sail and steam, running from landings situated where navigable waters neared high land. Some of the busiest wharves were Morley's, Concord, Shield's, and Rue's on Occohannock Creek.

The opening of the railroad, and the possibility of a spur line down Occohannock Neck, created competition between the railroad and local shippers. William J. Rue, who operated a wharf near Belle Haven, published a shipping schedule in the *Peninsula Enterprise*, the local weekly newspaper. In September 1885 Mr. Rue ran the following announcement:

> The safe delivery of every barrel of produce is guaranteed by me, the dangers of the sea excepted. Sort your potatoes well, fill your barrels full, and don't let the hot sun burn them at the time of digging them, ship them by my vessels according to my instructions, and I will guarantee satisfaction or as good returns as shipped by any other route. I will always be ready to buy at the wharf for cash or goods, and will pay the highest prices for good stock. Patronize your home friends.

One of the advantages of living and farming on a neck was that navigable water was near and accessible and there were always vessels to be had. Many farmers in Northampton County shipped their own potatoes simply by loading them onto private vessels and taking them to the railroad pier in Cape Charles City to sell directly to buyers.

When the market for white potatoes was at its strongest in the first decade of the 20th century, Cape Charles was a busy, thriving port, with a constant flow of vessels of all shapes and sizes bringing barrels of potatoes from the farm to the railroad. The peak of the white potato season was late June and early July, and the railroad during this time was shipping potatoes as fast as they could load them, which to some of the growers was not fast enough.

Peninsulas In Repose: The Necks of the Eastern Shore

On June 29, 1907 a writer with the *Norfolk Landmark* filed this report:

> On Thursday the New York, Philadelphia and Norfolk railroad sent out from that point (Cape Charles City) no less than 12,000 barrels, according to the shipping clerk's figures, and yesterday there were sent out almost as many. Still the cry is for more cars and some complain of the railroad, whether justly or not, for not handling them faster.
>
> There were one hundred sail vessels from Old Plantation, Hungars and Occohannock creeks anchored in the harbor awaiting their turn to unload yesterday afternoon. The greater number of these had to wait over until today. In the meantime, a large number of others constantly arrived until night fall.
>
> The farmers usually go down with the vessels and try to make sales on the dock. This in part accounts for the delay in handling the product. For this a potato exchange wharf would be a great convenience and it would enable the farmer to get his crop handled and at the same time relieve the congestion on the rail road wharf. Next week will see the biggest rush from this section.

The history of European settlement on Virginia's Eastern Shore is generally divided into periods ranging from early contact years, through formation of a society, the period of trade by sail, by steam, by railroad, and by highway. Our history has been marked by how we trade and how we travel, how we do business. These factors have determined where we live, what we grow and gather, and how we make profit from it. The necks of the Eastern Shore have been a part of all of these periods. Our necks, our peninsulas in repose, demonstrate that geology and geography play a great role in determining where we live and how we conduct trade and how we travel. The earliest setters were drawn to the necks because deep water made them accessible, and the fertile, sandy soil offered promise of wealth. And now, in our fifth century of settlement, we still find great value in our neck of the woods.

Neck Life

Life on the Eastern Shore centered on the water. It was part of everyday life. The tidal creeks, bays, and the ocean connected the Eastern Shore with the rest of the world. In addition, the creeks and bays were a great source of food, which fed the family and provided income. Most necks had at least one wharf, or pier, which acted as the focus for imports and exports. A few of these remain, but most are long gone, some sites marked only by a few pilings haphazardly arranged along a fringe of saltmarsh. The road signs are still there, the only tangible evidence of an earlier era. Evans Wharf Road, Boggs Wharf Road, Finneys Wharf Road, Morleys Wharf Road. Only the latter is still in the wharf business. Northampton County maintains a boat launch there, along with a popular fishing pier. Across Occohannock Creek from Morley's Wharf lies Davis Wharf, at the end of Davis Wharf Road, another port site that dates back centuries.

Eastern Shore necks, wooded areas of high land adjacent to navigable water, were the first lands to be settled by the English immigrants. There were necks on both the seaside and bayside, and the spine of the Eastern Shore, the area where commerce is centered today, was unfamiliar territory during the era of necks. When people visited the Eastern Shore, whether for commerce or social interaction, they came by water, did their business, and returned by water. There was little reason to explore the mid-woods beyond the community at the head of the neck.

Most of the early settlers came from the English countryside, and they brought with them many of the customs and manners of their native land. John S. Wise, son of Gov. Henry A. Wise, wrote in his memoir, *The End of an Era*, (Houghton, Mifflin Co. 1900) "Nowhere is the type of the original settler in Virginia so well preserved, or are to be found the antique customs, manners, and ways of the Englishman of the seventeenth century in America so little altered, as in the Kingdom of Accawmacke. No considerable influx of population from anywhere else has ever gone to the eastern shore of Virginia since the year 1700. The names of the very earliest settlers are still there."

Wise explained that the necks were created by creeks that separated the land by only a short distance in many places, but villages were separated by land often by great distances. "These numerous inlets, many of which are navigable for vessels of considerable size, are but a few miles apart, and divide the Peninsula into many transverse "necks," he wrote. "Thus, it often happens that neighbors living on opposite sides of these creeks, within hailing distance of each other, find it necessary, in order to visit each other by land, to travel miles around the head of the creek dividing them."

Wise noted that English names were used to identify necks and creeks on the southern part of the Eastern Shore, while native terms were used farther north. "On the bay side, going northward from the cape where the oldest settlements were made, the names of these creeks are English, such as Old Plantation, Cherrystone, and Hungars. Higher up the bay side, the names given by the Indians before the white settlements seem to have been retained; for we have successively Occohannock, Nandua, Pungoteague, Onancock, Chesconnessex, Annamessex, and Pocomoke as the names of the beautiful and bold insets on the bay side. On the sea side, they rejoice in such titles as Assawoman, Chincoteague, and the like."

The customs of the English survived a war of independence and various skirmishes since then, even to the present day. My family came from England and were farmers in Virginia, and I would bet they tilled the land back in whatever shire they left. My grandmother married a farmer and was the daughter of a farmer, and she brought English customs to her family farm on Red Bank Creek. She frequently referred to an area on the farm as the "pown yard," a word I had never heard before or since. She was speaking of the part of the farm separate from the formal yard and garden, but not part of the tilled land. In the pown yard were the barn and workshop, the equipment shed, corn crib, hen house, and various other structures critical to farming the land. The hog lot was in the pown yard as well, but situated a considerable distance from the house.

The necks are where ancient British customs gradually blended with new Eastern Shore ways and therefore became a distinctive part of our coastal culture. The ability to handle a boat was a given, and boat building became a distinct expression that brought together the practical needs of travel with the satisfaction of pleasing the eye. Boats were like duck decoys, made to please the eye and to perform a function. Wrote Wise: "Small boats are, therefore, as much in use as means of intercourse between neighbors, and for visiting the post offices and little towns at the wharves, as are horses and vehicles; and an eastern shore man is as much at home in a boat as upon the land."

A graphic example of the arrangement of necks, waterways, and villages can be found in old maps, most of which came from atlases of North America. The David Rumsey online collection (www.davidrumsey.com) includes numerous maps depicting Virginia and Maryland, and if you zoom in on particular maps, much detail can be seen. A map of Virginia, Maryland, and North Carolina was made by Johann Baptist Homann in 1720 and published in an atlas in Nuremberg, Germany. The necks are clearly delineated, especially on Northampton County's bayside, and are identified only by number, which probably references an accompanying text. The Eastern Shore of Virginia includes three counties – Northampton, Accomack, and Arcadia – and Virginia's Eastern Shore is shown as part of Maryland. No town names are given, but Teches Island (probably Parramore), Matthapunko Island (probably Hog), and Chincoteague Island are shown.

Also from the Rumsey collection is a map made by Henry S. Tanner in 1833 of Virginia, Maryland, and Delaware. Principal towns include Horntown, Drummondtown, Onancock, Pungoteague, Franktown, Kings Creek, Sand Hills, Bridgetown, and Belle Haven (which was spelled Beth Haven). Eastville, the county seat, was identified only by the number 164, which probably references to a guide in the atlas. No detail is shown of the central spine of the Eastern Shore, but a roadway is shown running north and south, which probably reflects guesswork on Tanner's part. It is obvious that cartographers were unfamiliar with the portion of the Eastern Shore away from the water, even as late as 1833. Local historian Brooks Miles Barnes says that during this period the central part of the Shore was, to most, *terra incognita*, unknown territory, a part of Virginia that remained generally unexplored long after the Revolution.

Tanner did know the seaside, though. He identified Assateague Island, Chincoteague, Wallops, Assawoman, Gargatha Inlet, Metompkin, Cedar, Little Machipongo Inlet, Hog, Revels, Upper Rack (Wreck) Island, Lower Rack, and Smith Island. No mention is made of Myrtle or Ship Shoal because they had not yet broken off from Smith Island.

A more modern map takes us to the dawn of the railroad era. It was made by Samuel A. Mitchell in 1884 and published in an atlas by William Bradley & Bro. of Philadelphia. The map features prominently the route of the NYP&N Railroad and the connecting routes of the Eastern Shore Railroad and Worcester Railroad in Maryand. More than thirty towns and villages were identified, but only Chincoteague and Cobbs Islands were recognized. The map was likely commissioned by Pennsylvania Railroad.

Eastern Shore towns prominently shown on maps in the pre-railroad era include some of our oldest communities, many of which were heads of necks or wharfs associated with necks. In Accomack, these include Pitt's Wharf, Horntown, Sandfordville (Sanford), Atlantic, Guilford (one of the oldest), Modest Town, Metompkin, Drummondtown, Locustville, Locust Mount, Hoffman's Wharf (Harborton), Belle Haven, and Davis Wharf.

In Northampton, from north to south, prominent communities include Hadlock, Concord Wharf, Wardtown, Franktown, Marionville, Bridgetown, Shady Side, Wilsonia Wharf, Eastville, Cherrystone, Sea View, and Capeville. Cape Charles City came along in 1884.

Towns and villages were named on many maps, but the location was often suspect. Franktown and Bridgetown, for example, although only a few miles apart on Bayside Road, roamed rather freely throughout upper Northampton County in early atlases.

Just as early maps provide a picture of what the Eastern Shore was like in pre-railroad days, so do written narratives. Many of the written records left by visitors are, predictably, accounts of visits to the barrier islands, usually for hunting and fishing trips. The Cobb family hotel opened just prior to the Civil War, and by 1870 or so was one of the most popular seaside resorts in the country. Accounts of visits to Cobbs Island were seen regularly in the outdoor press of the day. Alexander Hunter, a writer from Arlington, Virginia, was a regular hotel guest and wrote numerous stories about the seaside, many of which were included in his anthology *Huntsman in the South*, published in 1908. Other notable writers who covered the Shore include Rev. Thomas Dixon, who for a time lived in Cape Charles City and commuted by rail to a Baptist church in New York City, where he served as pastor. George Shiras was a congressman who championed some of America's first conservation legislation, and he had a home for nearly forty years on Revels Island. Shiras was a pioneering wildlife photographer, and his experiences on the Shore are chronicled in his two-volume set, *Hunting Wild Life with Camera and Flashlight*, published by the National Geographic Society.

Unfortunately, there are few written, descriptive accounts of visits to the *terra incognita* portion of the Eastern Shore prior to the opening of the railroad, and this leaves a void. Histories of the Eastern Shore are replete with dates and numbers and facts about land ownership, as well as laws passed and lawsuits filed and wills probated in the courts. These facts are important, of course, but they give little clue as to what people's lives were like, what they believed, what they did for fun, what their personalities were like. The reason for the void, naturally, is that few people set foot in *incognita land* other than permanent residents and their guests.

One who did was an artist from Wilmington, Delaware named Howard Pyle. A railroad linking the Shore with northern cities opened on April 7, 1876 when the Worcester Railroad christened a spur to Franklin City and thus gave birth to the great era of tourism on Chincoteague Island. Pyle was 23 and single at the time, an aspiring artist and writer who longed to escape his family's leather business in Wilmington. Pyle was educated at the Friends School and then studied art for three years with a Belgian artist named Van Der Weilen.

When news broke of the railroad link to Chincoteague, Pyle sensed an opportunity for adventure and a chance to launch a career as a freelance writer and illustrator. That spring or early summer, Pyle bought a train ticket for Franklin City, took a steamer to Chincoteague, and booked a room at the brand-new Atlantic Hotel for a few weeks.

Pyle spent his time making sketches and interviewing local people as he explored the island. As a result, his article on Chincoteague was published in *Scribner's Monthly* in 1877, along with eleven of his sketches. Through *Scribner's*, Pyle introduced Chincoteague to an audience that had been largely unfamiliar with the coastal island. *Scribner's* was one of the most popular magazines in America at the time, and it's fair to say that Chincoteague's current status as a tourist destination began with a rail spur, a steamboat ride, and a talented and ambitious young writer and illustrator from Wilmington, Delaware.

Pyle successfully avoided the leather business, moved to New York City, and soon became one of the best-known illustrators in the country. Pyle is credited as a founder of the "Brandywine School" of painting, which includes the noted artist, Andrew Wyeth.

Encouraged by the success of his work on Chincoteague, Pyle expanded his range and in May 1879 published an article in *Harper's New Monthly Magazine* titled A Peninsular Canaan, a sometimes fawning, sometimes acerbic look at what we today regard as the Delmarva Peninsula. Pyle describes the peninsula as a modern-day Canaan, a land of milk and honey, bypassed by modern times, clinging tenaciously to its old ways:

> One of the earliest English discoverers on this continent described the outlying Chesapeake shores of this peninsula, and its natural features have but little changed since that early time. When New York city was a wilderness inhabited by wild deer and Manhattoes, while Plymouth Rock all was still a virgin forest, Englishmen were growing tobacco, dredging oysters, and shooting wild fowl in this region. The vast tide of civilization has swept westward deluging the plains of Colorado southward to the chaparrals of Texas, and northward to the frozen shores of Alaska, but has left the peninsula still clinging to old manners

and customs, old modes of life and traditions with a firm tenacity. This is especially true the further southward one travels in this region, where, with but few exceptions, the descendants of the earlier settlers still live, with but a small increase of outside population. Separated from the outside world by the broad waters of the Delaware and Chesapeake, connected only by a narrow isthmus fifteen miles wide, with the body of the continent, one still finds here the easygoing old-time life, the broad hospitality of our forefathers, the careless air of ancient gentility, just tempered by an aristocratic exclusiveness. So the peninsula lies winking at the hurly-burly of modern progress, but it begins nevertheless at last to feel dubiously the intestine stir of modern Yankee notions in the midst of its indolent life.

For sixty-five miles of the lower length of the peninsula there is no railroad, and that in a country rich in natural products, easy of cultivation, and delightful in climate; there are but few steam saw or grist mills in a region abounding in valuable timber, and where corn meal is the staff of life; there are no steamboat lines on the Atlantic side, and but few on the Chesapeake, where almost the only means of being reached from the outside world is by water travel. Thus the southern peninsula, the garden spot of the country, to whose shore Nature seems to have invited man by every bounty she could lavish upon it, appears to be cut loose from the rest of the world, sleepily floating in the indolent sea of the past, incapable of crossing the gulf which separates it from outside modern life, and undesirous of joining in the race toward the wonderful future. *Requiescat in pace*, O Canaan of modern times, land overflowing with milk and honey, toward whose shores the footsteps of the pilgrim are directed *backward*! Who could visit thee and wish thee other than thou art?

While on the Eastern Shore of Virginia, Pyle visited Eastville, dined at the Eastville Inn, toured the office of the clerk of court, and then headed south to visit Custis Tomb at Arlington. He explored Hog Island, spending the night with a local family, and the next day witnessed an annual tradition on the island, the roundup and shearing of the sheep, which roamed freely over the island. He made numerous drawings during his visit, eleven of which were published in the magazine.

Peninsulas In Repose: The Necks of the Eastern Shore

Pyle's narrative swings like a pendulum, at one extreme lush with praise and appreciation for the natural gifts of the Shore, and at the other dismissive and condescending of the people who hosted him. Pyle ends his piece with this paragraph:

> The poor are wofully (sic) ignorant, and as the upper classes are, in many instances, indolently unprogressive, though far less so than formerly. In short, the Virginia portion of the peninsula seems sunk in a Rip Van Winkle sleep that has lasted a hundred instead of twenty years, and that as yet shows but small signs of awakening.

Pyle was a young man when he visited, still in his twenties and eager to make an impression. His narration is engaging and his descriptions testify to his skill in the visual arts, but now and then it seems the hormones kick in and Pyle sets off on some sort of adolescent riff that urges the reader to pay attention to the writer rather than the subject at hand. My guess is that if Pyle had revisited the manuscript in middle age, he would have done some editing.

Yet, Pyle had a point. The English settled first on the southern tip of the peninsula and gradually moved north as more immigrants settled on the Eastern Shore. By the 1630s, communities along the bay in Maryland were being settled, many of which reflect their English heritage and their place names. The northern part of the peninsula became the focus of industry, principally shipbuilding, with Harlan and Hollingsworth of Wilmington one of the busiest in the young country. Pyle grew up in Wilmington and was raised in an atmosphere of ambition and industry. Growth was good. Progressive citizens worked together and everyone benefitted. Indolence was slothful, a negative force within the community. It held back progress.

The lower Eastern Shore was rural and sparsely populated, as was most of eastern Virginia in the 17th and 18th centuries. There was little industry, but there were trades, most of which centered on either farming or fishing. Most settlers came from England and many were involved in indenture situations where they agreed to work for a skilled craftsman for a period of time in exchange for room, board, clothing, and instruction in a particular line of work. Historian Susie M. Ames called indenture "the original on-the-job training program in America."

For immigrants who could not afford passage from England to America, indentured servitude made the journey possible and also ensured work and shelter upon arrival in the new country. Many of the servants were indentured to planters. Sometimes indenture was made by the father on behalf of a son. Ames, in her book *Studies of the Virginia Eastern Shore in the 17th Century*, gave the example of James Lee and Peter Pritchard of Accomack regarding Pritchard's son, Joseph, who wanted to learn the trade of tailor. Joseph Pritchard agreed to serve Lee for four years and three months in order to learn the trade. Lee would provide food, clothing, and shelter to Joseph during the period of indenture and give Lee some tools of the trade when the indenture ended.

In 1696, arrangements were made for Reginald Eyre, the eldest son of Benjamin and Martha Eyre, to live with Thomas Bonewell to learn the trade of a blacksmith. John Sharpley of Accomack County bound his son John to George Key, shoemaker, "the said Key to instruct John Sharpley in the art and trade of shoe making or cordwinder." Indentures were legal agreements and were recorded in court orders in both counties.

Indentures were not restricted to the working classes. "Since apprenticeship was about the only means of securing industrial training at that time, it was sometimes sought by individuals fairly fortunate as regards birth and material possessions," wrote Ames.

Consider the case of the Parramores, one of the more noted families of the Eastern Shore who owned a plantation called *Bellevue* on the seaside southeast of Accomac. The Parramores fought in the American Revolution and later served the community as judges, doctors, and elected officials. The first Parramore came to America as an indentured servant, but by the time of the Revolution the family was among the leaders of the growing Virginia colony.

John Parramore arrived in 1622 aboard the *Bona Venture* as a 17-year-old servant to John Blower. By the 1630s Parramore's name was appearing regularly in court documents, ranging in nature from litigation over business transactions to a charge of cursing on the Sabbath. By the early 1640s, Parramore was thriving to the point where he had an indentured servant of his own, Edward Robins.

By 1650 Parramore was living on a 200-acre plantation in Northampton County on Magothy Bay. He later bought a 250-acre farm on Occohannock Creek on the Chesapeake Bay. On November 9, 1666, Parramore patented 1,500 acres in northern Accomack County near the Maryland line, and then had to repeat the patent process with Maryand in 1668 when Virginia gave up its claim to the area. Parramore thus named the plantation "Double Purchase." He died there in 1676.

Many descriptions of the Eastern Shore in the pre-railroad days depict the peninsula as rural and poor. The necks were decidedly rural, but to describe the people as poor begs the question, "relative to what?" Howard Pyle on one hand describes the landscape as verdant and lush, providing a bounty from both land and sea. Yet the people are woefully ignorant, indolent, and unprogressive.

The people of the necks lived closely with the land and the sea and by some standards could be described as poor, if your definition of the term involves bank balances and investment portfolios. They could be described as ignorant if a measure of knowledge involves Greek classics. They could be unprogressive if progressive means being unsatisfied with your current lot in life and in constant need of something newer and better.

Neck Business

The first industry on the Eastern Shore was salt making. Salt was needed to preserve fish and other foods for use during times when things were scarce. During the first years of the Jamestown Colony, many people died of starvation and disease. The colony turned to the Eastern Shore for the precious crystals that would help them survive a winter.

Salt was made by heating sea water until the liquid was vaporized, leaving a crusty layer of crystals. The colony sent a small group of men to the tip of the Eastern Shore peninsula, where they set up salt making facilities on Smith and Mockhorn Islands. The sea water was sometimes heated in large vats with a fire built below, and salt was also derived from the simple process of evaporation by the sun. The men lived on the mainland in an encampment called Dale's Gift, where they also grew corn, squash, and other vegetables for the Jamestown settlement.

Dale's Gift was the creation of acting governor Sir Thomas Dale, and theories vary as to its exact location, and to the origin of the name. Some say it originated with the crew assigned to the outpost, and was intended with some degree of sarcasm. Here was a small band of men, virtually unarmed, without protection, sent to evaporate sea water in a remote location believed to be populated by armed natives. Some gift.

Salt was also made in the necks. Saltworks were located on the shores of Nassawadox Creek on Occohannock Neck. Nothing remains of the facility, but Saltworks Road still connects Jamesville with the site of the saltworks on the creek. The saltworks on Occohannock Neck were built by Col. Edmund Scarburgh around 1660, according to Susie M. Ames, who wrote that Scarburgh also had saltworks on his property in Gargaphia Neck in Accomack County.

Salt was a precious commodity and its price was fixed by the government at thirty pounds of tobacco per bushel of salt. Persons guilty of charging more, of price gouging, were fined substantial amounts to protect the public interest.

Tobacco was the first item to be traded widely and it was a major crop in the necks of the Eastern Shore. By 1632, so much tobacco was being produced in the colony that the governor issued a proclamation limiting each grower to no more than one-thousand plants. Eastern Shore products early on were shipped to the Western Shore and from there to England, but by the mid-1600s warehouses were built on local creeks and tobacco was shipped directly to Europe. Tobacco warehouses were originally built in Northampton at Kings Creek and

Plantation Creek, and later at Cherrystone, Nassawadox, and Hungars. Warehouses in Accomack were on Pungoteague Creek, Guilford Creek, and Pitt's Creek. The tobacco warehouse era is still reflected in place names. Warehouse Prong is a stream at the head of Pungoteague Creek, and on nearby upland is a street called Warehouse Road.

The leadership of the Jamestown Colony largely controlled the shipping of goods, with England being the primary export destination. The Eastern Shore's remote location, however, allowed local shippers more leeway in determining where products were headed. According to Susie M. Ames, the Eastern Shore enjoyed a certain independence of commerce, frequently doing business with the Dutch. Records show that tobacco was being shipped along the coast to New Netherlands and New England from the Eastern Shore, circa 1650.

The tobacco era began to wane around 1660 to 1670 for a variety of reasons, mainly because of poor markets and falling prices. But Ames believes there were two other reasons for the demise of the tobacco market: the exhaustion of the soil and the fact that there was no longer much free land available. "By the close of the century most of the area of the Eastern Shore had been patented, and the large plantations of the preceding generation were being partitioned to an increasing population," Ames wrote in *Studies of the Virginia Eastern Shore in the 17th Century*.

"By 1715 there was so little interest in tobacco that Accomack petitioned the Assembly that its inhabitants might pay their public dues in pork, beef, wheat and other country commodities; but the proposition was rejected."

The tobacco era on the Eastern Shore was succeeded by a shift to grain and livestock. The transition was relatively seamless, according to Ames. "The comparative ease with which the transition was made may be attributed in part to the fact that it occurred before the influx of slaves into the colony during the eighteenth century, but primarily to the fact that there had been an early and continuous interest in grain and livestock and that geographical factors had fostered inter-colonial marketing. The first settlers had engaged in a diversified agriculture and, on the basis of its products, had built up a profitable trade along the Atlantic seaboard. So the decline of tobacco culture did not mean the centering of attention upon unknown commodities; it meant merely the expansion of a trade already established in other agricultural products."

Businesses and artisanal crafts on the Eastern Shore included the grinding of grain to make bread, and most necks had at least one water mill at the head of a creek. People had orchards to produce fruit, cider, and brandy, peach being a favorite. Craftsmen made bricks for construction projects using clay found near the shores of creeks. Furniture making, weaving, shoemaking, blacksmithing, and shipbuilding were all skills employed by people living in the necks.

The Planter, Mariner, and Merchant

The Eastern Shore's easy access to water clouded the sharp line that in other cultures divided occupations and skills. A planter might also be a mariner or a merchant, depending upon the season and the business at hand. Many planters who worked the necks of the Eastern Shore frequently had a privately owned vessel moored nearby.

Eastern Shore people are known to have an amphibious quality – equally at home on land and water. Consider my great-grandfather, John Badger, and his older brother, Thomas. Like many young men in America in 1849, they dreamed of striking it rich in the gold fields of California. Their father had died in 1846 when Thomas was 19, and he had become the leader of the family. At 15, he had taken a job as a mate on a cargo vessel, and thus began his life as a seaman.

In 1848 word spread around the world that James Marshall had discovered gold near Sutter's Fort in California. Suddenly, men by the tens of thousands took off to seek fortune and adventure in the gold fields of the west. Some traveled across country and others came by boat. Thomas and John were both experienced sailors, so they chose the latter method. They left their home port of Red Bank and sailed north to New York, and on March 3, 1849 they boarded the schooner

James L. Day for California. They sailed from New York around Cape Horn and then took a northern route up the coast. The journey took nearly six months. Thomas was 22 and John was about a month shy of 17.

Thomas remained in California for most of his life, and John eventually returned to the farm on Red Bank Creek. It is not known whether they found gold, but the experience had a profound effect on their lives. John became a planter, but he also was a mariner, and, when the opportunity presented itself, he was a merchant. John owned the schooner *Louisiana* during the years prior to the Civil War, and the *Panama* following the war. A story passed down through the family holds that Captain John got caught running a blockade during the war and forfeited the *Louisiana* to the Union navy. The *Panama* replaced it.

Family records show that John did regular business in New York and Boston, shipping produce grown on his own farm and that of others, and he seldom returned from trips to northern cities carrying ballast. Furniture, kitchenware, musical instruments, clothing, and tools were frequently stowed in the hold. John also did business in the West Indies, usually shipping corn, barrels of pork, pitch, tar, and lumber to the islands and returning with rum, sugar, molasses, and cocoa.

The Eastern Shore might be unique in marrying the roles of planter and mariner. The conventional wisdom is that once a mariner patents land, clears acreage, builds a shelter, fences in a pasture, and acquires livestock to care for, he in due course gives up the sea. But on the Eastern Shore, once the vast tracts patented during the early years were broken up, most farms were of a modest size – one hundred acres or so -- and a landowner could spend time at sea marketing his goods as well as behind the plow during the growing season.

Captain John was among the last to play this role. His prime years were just before and after the Civil War, and when the railroad came in the 1880s he was one of many planter-mariner-merchants on the Eastern Shore to see their careers end. It was a system that dated back to the earliest days of settlement. For mariners who settled on the Eastern Shore, the sea was never far from their thoughts, or far from their farmsteads. John had sailed around Cape Horn when he was 16;

he would never be intimidated by going to sea.

Among the first of the planter-mariners was John Wallop, who patented 1,700 acres in northern Accomack County, what we know today as Wallops Neck and Wallops Island. Wallop successfully combined his career as a mariner with that of a planter, despite the vast acreage he oversaw.

According to Susie M. Ames, Robert Pitt in 1662 and 1663 patented 4,000 acres in northwest Accomack, a tract bordered by the Pocomoke River on the north, and on the west by the Chesapeake Bay and by "sunken marshes called Pitt's Neck." He and his son grew crops on the land and distributed them in vessels of their own.

"The seafaring man might become a landholder and planter, but if that land had a water location, the call of the sea did not go unheeded," wrote Ames.

Bars and Ordinaries

Prior to the railroad days, the closest thing the Eastern Shore had to towns and villages – other than the two county seats – were the communities that often sprouted at the heads of the necks. While the necks centered on production and trade, most were linked by facilities shared in common. At the head of the neck would be a community of churches, stores, inns, bars, blacksmiths, tanneries, and perhaps an apothecary.

At the head of Church Neck is Hungars Church, founded in 1623 in a village that would become known as Bridgetown. Shady Side was the head of Wilsonia Neck. At the head of Wellington Neck is the village of Franktown, which had stores, inns, and churches to serve both Black and White. The post office delivered mail to Franktown and Bridgetown, where people who lived down the neck could come to collect their correspondence. These communities, these nascent villages, were linked to each other by horse and buggy trails, one on the bayside and one on the seaside.

A common feature of the head of the neck would be the bar or ordinary, the American equivalent of the British public house. The first ordinary was licensed by Anthony Hodgskins on Old Plantation Creek and it did duty not only as a pub and inn, but as the county court as well. By the 1800s bars and ordinaries were so numerous, applications for liquor licenses were a standard part of the monthly court proceedings.

Many of the place names were left behind when people emigrated from the necks to railroad towns in the late 19th and early 20th centuries. Court proceedings from October 1881 listed four new bars being licensed: to Richard P. Read at Hoffman's Wharf, James S. Nock at Assawoman, Frank P. McConnell at Chincoteague Island, and to Eli W. Bull at Bull Run (today, Daugherty). Hoffman's Wharf, now Harborton, was an appendage of Hacks Neck, Assawoman the head of Arbuckle Neck, and Bull Run the head of Custis Neck.

The court in its June 1882 session granted licenses to Louis S. Belote at Fair Oaks (Melfa), George A. Fowler at both Hawk's Nest (Mappsburg) and Sycamore Turn (probably Sycamore Bend on Finneys Creek), to Louis F. Hinman at Hunting Creek, and Revel C. Taylor at Guilford Wharf.

Licensing bars and retail sellers was an important source of revenue for the county governments, and the court took it seriously when someone flouted the law. In the May 1883 court session, Judge Thomas C. Parramore sentenced W. S. Waterman to five days in the county jail and a fine of $18.36 for selling liquor without a license.

The court also regarded liquor and gambling as partners in crime. In July 1882, William T. Barnes and his business partners pleaded guilty to a charge of unlawful gambling at their house of entertainment at Hunting Creek, paid a fine of $115.17, and forfeited their bar room license.

The bars and ordinaries (which offered overnight accommodations) were an important part of the social fabric of the pre-railroad Eastern Shore. Saturday night at the head of the neck was a weekend celebration that ended the work week on a high note. By the time the railroad rolled in, the court was considering dozens of license applications in each session. Some of the bars would be in traditional places of business, others simply in a spare room in an applicant's home.

Many local residents made their own sprits of choice. Farms of the 19th century were diverse, and most included scuppernong grapes for making wine and peach orchards for making brandy.

Capt. John grew peaches for making brandy on his Red Bank farm. His brother Tom, who lived in California, wrote to him in January 1876 and requested a keg of peach brandy. "Ship it express from Baltimore as soon as you can," he asked, "but put the keg inside of another keg. Otherwise, someone will draw the brandy off and replace it with water."

Saturday Night at the Head of the Neck

The following account was written by Thomas G. Elliott of Accomac and was published in the August 5, 1880 issue of *Forest & Stream* magazine. It is a good example of how people who lived in the necks entertained themselves. Obviously, there was no radio, television, or internet, and in 1880 the number of people who could read for pleasure were a minority. So, the store or the ordinary at the head of the neck would be a place for the men to gather and tell stories and to perhaps have a nip of "old tangle-foot."

> There was a great meeting of the "Neckers" at our store last Saturday night. After the boys had spun their yarns, in good order, some dropping quail in crossing a four-foot path, resting their arms on fence rails, killing with their guns "kicking up behind and before," bagging coons, opossums, etc., etc., Uncle Mike Jones put in an appearance by stating that his father had often related to him the prowess of his grandfather in the use of a gun, which he had imported from Holland, known as "the old pewter piece," and, amongst other things, described his wholesale destruction of blackbirds on one occasion, when he swung her around an oat stack, and killed all the way around, the charge terminating in taking off the skirts of his long-tailed blue, whereupon, being an ardent admirer of old "tangle-leg," he proposed a drink.
>
> John Bush, whose inclinations had turned, for several years, toward the "biled owl" fraternity, having been a great listener,

put in a word, which he said in no way was meant as disputing the flexibility, under curved pressure, of the gun of Mike's progenitor, stated that he, on one occasion, had made a shot somewhat alarming to tell, yet, as there still walked two living witnesses, he would relate that the occasion did not arise by putting his piece in a circular attitude, but that he held it straight from the shoulder, and left dead on the sand 350 assorted birds, curlew, snipe, etc., and, in candor, believed that as many more fluttered off, wounded, on the water.

Uncle Mike spoke up and asked: "If but one barrel?" "Only one." "What size shot?" "Fours." "Two ounce charge?" "About." "Will some gentleman be so good as to count if there are 700 pellets of fours in two ounces."

Now, you see that things began to look rather "cornerfied" for John, and as the old "tangle-foot" was working up to the usual standard, it was plain that something must be done, for the double purpose of staving off muscular action, and to drive the two heroes of the evening to an alliance, and nothing short of the "Western Farmer" could accomplish that end, so Cousin Burton stated that on one occasion a Western farmer had done wonders without good results, and he would be glad to have their attention to hear it.

Silence having been reached, this old coon hunter went on to say that this farmer had constructed a level floor for the purpose of baiting wild pigeons, and after alluring them to his place in great numbers concluded he had better secure some profits for his outlay. With a double charge in his old fusil he lashed it to two posts and lay in wait. When all things were ready, and pigeons had come in such numbers as to lead him to anticipate the need of a wagon to carry off the dead, he gave a grunt to start the birds on the wing, and pulled the cord, when lo! not one bird was left prostrated on the field, having pulled too late by one and three-quarter inches.

"Well," says Mike, "nothing very remarkable about that."

"But I was going to say that he swept up nine and half bushels of legs and feet."

"Oh! Come, John, come, s'pose we have just one nip and go."

"I don't want any, " said Bush; "that pigeon affair is all that I can carry."

Chapter 18:
The Nature Conservancy

I brought home my first wild game when I was fourteen. The birds were marsh hens, or clapper rail, and I was with my father in a little cedar skiff in a flooded salt marsh near Cedar Island. The moon was full and the wind was northeast, pushing the tide high into the marsh, covering the grasses where the rails hid. They would dart nervously among the spindly blades of cordgrass, reluctantly taking flight as we nudged the skiff into a tump of grass. By the time the day ended, we had a dozen or so for dinner.

At the time, it seemed an enjoyable but unremarkable day, another item in a catalog of events that were a part of growing up on the coast. I had caught flounder by drifting baits of minnow and squid along a channel in a shallow bay. I had learned to find clams on a tidal flat at low tide. I had walked miles of ocean beach, wild as it was when the First People came to collect whelks buried in the sand. And it all seemed unremarkable and not at all special.

I didn't value this life, this experience, until the day I sensed it was slipping away. I had grown up, gone to college, and was working as a photojournalist in the air force in Alaska. My hometown newspaper arrived one day in June 1969, bringing news that a New York developer called Smith Island Development Corporation had bought three islands and intended to link them by bridge to the mainland and build a golf course, a residential community to accommodate 50,000 people, retail shops, and restaurants. This news suddenly assigned currency to a way of life I had not considered as having any exceptional value, in much the way the value of life is not thoughtfully measured until life is threatened.

I had never heard of The Nature Conservancy until my newspaper reported that the organization had bought an island near the proposed development and planned to preserve it in its natural state. In the ensuing months there was great debate about economic development, the need for jobs, and the importance of preserving a natural legacy. In December 1970 news came that TNC had purchased the three islands from the developers and that the development was off. To me, the arrival of TNC was like the cavalry riding in just as the bad guys were holding up the stage. I could hear the bugles blow.

That was the beginning of the Virginia Coast Reserve, one of the first and most significant land protection programs by TNC in Virginia. Since then, TNC has spent more than fifty years protecting land on the Eastern Shore and throughout Virginia. From the Clinch Valley in southwest Virginia to the Allegheny Highlands and Warm Springs Mountain, to Piney Grove in southeast Virginia and throughout the Chesapeake Bay watershed, TNC has helped protect more than 500,000 acres.

Michael Lipford, the director of The Nature Conservancy in Virginia when these programs were being put in place, still considers the Virginia Coast Reserve the state's signature project. "These islands, bays, and marshes are the last of the coastal wilderness along the mid-Atlantic," says Lipford. "This wasn't an issue of rescue or restoration, it was preservation of an ecosystem in its original and unaltered state. Opportunities like that don't come along very often."

The Nature Conservancy assembled a preserve of about 45,000 acres on fourteen barrier islands, quite an achievement for an organization that began with a tiny membership base and little national clout among conservation organizations. There is a story that the early organizers of TNC met around a kitchen table and kept the membership list on note cards stored in a shoebox. In Virginia, the state chapter was created in a private residence in Richmond. "The Conservancy in Virginia literally began in Elizabeth Bocock's living room on Franklin Street," says Lipford. "State senator Fitzgerald Bemiss was there, as was attorney George Clemon Freeman, Jr. and Richard Pough, who was president of The Nature Conservancy nationally. It was strictly a volunteer organization. There was no paid staff for the first twenty-five years."

Growth of The Nature Conservancy nationally and on the state level began at a time when there was an increasing awareness that we have a responsibility to be good stewards of the land. The government was getting serious about legislation to protect tidal wetlands, and the centuries-long practice of filling and draining marshes was about to come to an end.

The Nature Conservancy provided a private means of protecting land to complement the public efforts of state and federal governments. The partnership worked well because, unburdened by bureaucracy, TNC could act quickly. If an important tract of land became available, TNC was agile enough to step in and take action. A good example would be a large tract in the Great Dismal Swamp, which TNC acquired from the Union Camp Corporation, and later turned over to the Department of Fish and Wildlife to create the Great Dismal Swamp National Wildlife Refuge.

In the early days, TNC's method of protecting land was simple and direct. It identified special places that needed protection, and it bought them. In the case of the Virginia barrier islands, TNC had a like-minded partner with significant resources in the Mary Flagler Cary Charitable Trust of New York. The trust invested more than $20 million in protecting the barrier island ecosystem of the Eastern Shore.

One of the early lessons of conservation of natural areas is the realization that all things are connected. An island is not in and of itself. It is part of a system of islands. And the islands are affected by what happens on the mainland, and by what happens in the waterways that surround them.

Pat Noonan, who later became president of The Nature

Conservancy, joined the organization when negotiations were just getting underway to assemble the Virginia Coast Reserve. Noonan invited Ed Bentley, a Cary Trustee, to visit some of the islands by boat. As Noonan was cautiously sounding Bentley out about a modest grant to buy a limited site, Bentley became impatient and interrupted Noonan several times to ask him who owned the neighboring island, and the one after that, and the one farther south...

Noonan calmly raised his sights, adjusted his pitch, and the idea of protecting an entire barrier island ecosystem had begun.

Correspondence from the early days of the TNC/Cary Trust relationship indicates the depth of feeling both sides had for the project. Following his trip to the islands with Pat Noonan, Ed Bentley wrote a letter to fellow trustee Herb Jacobi on October 12, 1971:

"While we landed only on Parramore Island, Cedar Island, and an oyster bar off Metompkin Island, and spent most of our time on the marshes, the land and the marsh areas that we visited were representative of the entire area in which we are interested, and indeed the entire area from Chincoteague to Cape Charles.

"The impressions that I received were overpowering, particularly when I realized what we, as Mary's trustees, had been able to accomplish in preserving the area that we were visiting, as well as what remained to be done, and what we hoped to undertake in the future."

It quickly became apparent that any attempt to provide long term protection to a diverse natural area would require teamwork and partnerships. The Nature Conservancy's strong relationship with the Cary Trust was vital, but it was just the beginning. Partnerships within the community were important too.

It had long been recognized that the Virginia portion of the Delmarva Peninsula was a vital resting and feeding stop for migrating birds. As they migrated south in the fall, songbirds would gather in great numbers at the southern tip of the peninsula before making the seventeen-mile crossing of the Chesapeake Bay. To provide long term protection for the birds, it would be necessary to protect the natural communities of the southern tip.

Over the years, this has been accomplished through a number of partnerships. The former army base, Fort John Custis, at the tip of the peninsula, is now protected as the Eastern Shore of Virginia National Wildlife Refuge. Neighboring Fisherman Island is also a wildlife refuge. The state has created natural area preserves on the seaside at Magothy Bay, and on the bayside at Pickett's Harbor, just north of Kiptopeke State Park. The barrier islands are protected through federal, state, and TNC ownership.

The mainland Eastern Shore is part of the migration corridor, and farms and woodland are being protected through conservation easements that ensure the landscape will retain its agricultural and light residential use. The Nature Conservancy used Cary Trust grants to buy a number of seaside farms, and then sold the farms to private individuals with easements attached that ensure compatible land use. Community organizations such as the Eastern Shore Land Trust have protected thousands of acres of farms and woodland through conservation easements.

The use of easements not only protects land for migrating birds, it protects water quality as well, supporting the growth of the clam and oyster aquaculture industries as well as conventional seafood harvesting.

One of the more dramatic restoration efforts on the seaside has taken place in Northampton County, where TNC is working with partners to reestablish sea grass beds in the shallow coastal bays. The grass beds, and the shellfish that depend on them for shelter, were wiped out by storms and blight in the 1930s and are returning today. Hundreds of volunteers have donned masks and snorkels to harvest seed-bearing pods in the spring. Once the seeds mature over the summer, they are extracted from the pods and broadcast over the shallow bays to augment natural growth.

I grew up on the Eastern Shore, graduated from Onancock High School, and had no idea that I lived in a natural area that was in any way special. Our high school was tucked into a bend of Onancock Creek and we could look out the windows and watch the rising and falling of the tide. A few miles downstream, Onancock Creek joined the Chesapeake Bay. Spartina marshes were so close to the baseball field that they frequently swallowed up foul balls. We were going to school in a striped bass nursery. Yet, in biology class, we dissected pickled frogs purchased from a biological supply house in North Carolina.

There simply was no awareness that salt marshes and freshwater wetlands held any value. We dumped our trash in them. When our school was built in 1921 they made a football field by hauling truckloads of fill to the edge of the marsh and dumping it. They hauled and dumped until the marsh was covered, and then they packed it down and hauled and dumped some more. A small sandy beach was downstream from school and our parents urged us to avoid it. Shit Beach, it was called. It was a product of Onancock's waste treatment system of the day. The tide comes in. The tide goes out.

It is rewarding, then, to tag along when TNC's education staff takes a group of third graders out to explore a salt marsh or a tidal flat at low tide. Children take delight in learning about life, dragging a minnow seine along a beach to catch grass shrimp and killifish, finding clam sign exposed at low water, and then using bare hands to discover what lies below.

In learning about life, they are learning the importance of landscape, the need to protect and preserve the whole of it. It all matters, even the smallest creature, and they need to know they are living in a remarkable place and having a remarkable and unique experience. This life does have currency, and, indeed, it should be thoughtfully measured. It still could all slip away.

BIBLIOGRAPHY

Ames, Susie M.
The Company's Garden: Dale's Gift
Hickory House, 1998

Ames, Susie M.
Studies of the Virginia Eastern Shore in the Seventeenth Century
The Dietz Press, Richmond, Virginia 1940

Badger, Curtis J.
Salt Tide – Cycles and Currents of Life Along the Coast
Countryman Press, 1999

Badger, Tom and Curtis Badger
Images of America – Accomack County
Arcadia, 2009

Badger, Tom and Curtis Badger
Images of America – Northampton County
Arcadia, 2011

Badger, Curtis J.
Bellevue Farm – Exploring Virginia's Coastal Countryside
Stackpole Books, 1997

Bibliography

Barnes, Brooks Miles and Barry R. Truitt
Seashore Chronicles – Three Centuries of the Virginia Barrier Islands
University of Virginia Press, 1997

Barnes, Brooks Miles and William G. Thomas
The Countryside Transformed: The Railroad and the Eastern Shore of Virginia, 1870-1935. A Collaborative Effort of the Eastern Shore of Virginia Public Library and the Virginia Center for Digital History of the University of Virginia, 2008.

Blanton, Dennis B.
A Study of First People of the Eastern Shore
William & Mary Center for Archaeological Research, 1999

Doughty, L.E.
A Narrative About Life on Hog Island, Va.
Hickory House, 2002

Egloff, Keith and Deborah Woodward
First People – The Early Indians of Virginia
Virginia Department of Historic Resources, 1992

Gingerich, Joseph A.M.
In the Eastern Fluted Point Tradition, Vol. 2
University of Utah Press, 2017

Hunter, Alexander
Huntsman in the South
Neale Publishing Company, 1908

Hurley, George and Suzanne
Shipwrecks and Rescues Along the Barrier Islands of Delaware, Maryland, and Virginia
Donning, 1984

Kagawa, Ron M. and Richard Kellam
Cobb's Island, Virginia, The Last Sentinel
The Donning Company, 2003

Krieger, Robert L.
The Life and Times of Benjamin Franklin Scott, 1838 – 1944
Appendix B to an as yet unwritten book, 1979

Kurlansky, Mark
The Big Oyster – History on the Half Shell
Random House 2006

Mangum, Richard and Sherry
One Woman's West – The Life of Mary-Russell Ferrell Colton
Northland Publishing, 1997

Mariner, Kirk
Once Upon an Island
Miona Publications, 2003

Mears, James Egbert
Hacks Neck and Its People, Past and Present
Privately published, 1937

Newberry, S. Lloyd
Wings of Wonder – The Remarkable Story of the Cobb Family and the Priceless Decoys They Created on Their Island Paradise
Sporting Classics, 2020

Perry, James R.
The Formation of a Society on Virginia's Eastern Shore, 1615-1655
University of North Carolina Press, 1990

Bibliography

Pouliot, Richard C. and Julie J.
Shipwrecks on the Virginia Coast and the Men of the Life-Saving Service
Tidewater Publishers, 1986

Rountree, Helen C. and Thomas E. Davidson
Eastern Shore Indians of Virginia and Maryland
University of Virginia Press, 1997

Shiras, George 3d
Hunting Wild Life with Camera and Flashlight
National Geographic Society, 1935

Shomette, Donald G.
Shipwrecks, Sea Raiders, and Maritime Disasters along the Delmarva Coast 1632-2004
The Johns Hopkins University Press, 2007

Smith, Clint
How the Word is Passed
Little, Brown and Company

Sterling, Charles A.
Hog Island Virginia
Hickory House reprint of 1903 original, privately published

Teal, John and Mildred
Life and Death of the Salt Marsh
Little, Brown and Company, 1969

Thoreau, Henry David
Cape Cod
Penguin Books, 1987

Whitelaw, Ralph T.
Virginia's Eastern Shore – A History of Northampton and Accomack Counties
Peter Smith, 1968

Wigeon, Yvonne Marshall
Precious Memories of Childhood Days on Hog Island
Privately published

Wise, John Sergeant
The End of an Era
Houghton, Mifflin and Company, 1899

Index

A

Accocomson Island 28
Accomac 34, 36, 53, 54, 55, 59, 101, 112, 126, 140, 152, 160
Accomac Club vii, viii, 28, 41, 42, 50, 52, 53, 57, 127
Accomack County 16, 18, 25, 30, 40, 52, 53, 56, 62, 63, 105, 115, 135, 139, 140, 146, 147, 152, 153, 154, 155, 158
Accomacks (tribe) 10, 68
A History of the Cobb Family 100
Allie B. Chester 127
American Fish Guano Company 38
American Revolution 62, 63, 69, 75, 147, 152
Ames, Susie M. 152, 154, 155, 158
A Narrative About Life on Hog Island, Va. 67
Andean 114
Andrews, Jack 127
Angibaud, Louis-Andre 37, 38
Annamessex Creek 145
Arbuckle Neck 159
Arcadia 146
Argoll, Samuel 104, 109
Arlington 58, 110, 111, 148, 150
Arlington National Cemetery 110
Assateague Beach 125
Assateague Island v, vi, 1, 3, 14, 15, 16, 19, 20, 21, 22, 23, 24, 27, 33, 34, 38, 39, 59, 66, 69, 70, 147
Assateague Island National Seashore 14
Assawoman 31, 145, 147, 159
Atlantic 147
Atlantic Hotel 21, 149
Aunt Caroline 46

B

Badger, John 156, 157, 160
Badger, Thomas 156, 157, 160
Baileys Neck 140
Baltimore and Ohio Railroad 128
Baltimore, Maryland 23, 37, 63, 114, 128, 160
Baltimore Sun 99, 101, 114
Barnes, Brooks Miles 73, 110, 137, 146
Bayview 18
Belle Haven 142, 146, 147
Bellevue 62, 63, 152
Bells Neck 136
Benson, G.W. 114
Bentley, Ed 165

Bird Islands 113
Birdsnest ix
Blanton, Dennis 10, 11
Bona Venture 62, 152
brant 71, 72, 74, 88, 101
breeches buoy 125, 132
Bridgetown 146, 147, 158
Broadwater 4, 64, 77, 82, 137, 139
Broadwater Club i, ii, vii, 28, 78, 80, 81, 82, 86, 87, 88
Broadwater Inlet 88
Broadwater Island 75, 77, 78, 79, 80, 81, 82, 87
Broadwater Land and Improvement Company i, vii, 64, 76, 80, 81
Broadwater Oyster Association 78
Broadwater pier 79
Broadway Neck 140
Browne, Orris A. 38, 39
Browne's Superior Cedar Island Guano 38
Budd, George 119
Budd, Jenny 119, 120
Bullbeggar Creek 136
Bull Run 159
Burtons Bay 1
Burtons Shore 35
Burwell, Nellie Field 24

C

Californian 114
Campbell, Samuel O. 111
Cape Charles 113, 115, 118, 131, 139, 142, 165
Cape Charles City 142, 143, 147, 148
Cape Charles Lighthouse 105, 110
Cape Charles Quarantine Station 115, 116, 118
Cape Henry 118, 131
Capeville 147
Carson, Rachael L. 112

Cary, Mary Flagler 51, 65, 165
Cashville 138
Cashville Cornet Band 53
Cattail Neck 140
Cedar Island 1, 33, 34, 35, 36, 38, 39, 125, 127, 147, 162, 165
Cedar Island Life-Saving Station 127
Charles Foster 117
Cherrystone 147, 155
Cherrystone Creek 138, 145
Cherrystone Inlet 138
Cherrystone Landing 94
Cherrystone Wharf 105
Chesapeake Bay vii, 3, 10, 38, 62, 83, 109, 110, 115, 116, 117, 118, 120, 134, 137, 138, 141, 149, 150, 153, 158, 163, 167
Chesapeake Bay Bridge-Tunnel 110, 113, 121
Chesapeakes (tribe) 10
Chesapeake Watershed Archaeological Research Foundation 12
Chesconnessex Creek 145
Chesser, Grayson 94
Chincoteague Baptist Church 16
Chincoteague Bay ii, 16, 18, 21, 25, 26, 33, 135
Chincoteague Island ii, iii, 14, 15, 16, 17, 18, 20, 21, 22, 23, 24, 25, 26, 27, 28, 29, 30, 33, 38, 43, 50, 51, 67, 69, 77, 98, 146, 147, 148, 149, 159, 165
Chincoteague National Wildlife Refuge 24
Chincoteague Naval Air Station 30
Chincoteague oysters 14
Chincoteague ponies 15, 19, 21, 22, 79, 81
Chincoteagues (tribe) 16
Chincoteague Volunteer Fire Company 17, 22

cholera viii, 114, 116, 118
Church Creek 136
Church Neck 136, 158
Civil War vi, 18, 30, 47, 48, 63, 64, 92, 94, 95, 101, 105, 110, 113, 122, 123, 148, 157
Cleveland, Grover vii, 64, 66, 78, 82, 86, 87, 88, 89, 90, 91, 133
Clovis people 12, 13, 104
Cobb, Albert 93
Cobb-Butler Shipbuilding Company 99, 100
Cobb Cottage 98
Cobb family vi, ix, 73, 82, 93, 94, 95, 96, 97, 99, 101, 148
Cobb, Francis 99, 100
Cobb, George 83
Cobb, Nancy 92
Cobb, Nathan Farwell 100
Cobb, Nathan Fosque Jr. 93, 94
Cobb, Nathan Fosque Sr. 92, 93, 94, 96, 97, 98, 99, 100, 101, 102, 105
Cobb, Phillip L. 100
Cobbs Island vi, viii, ix, 30, 35, 82, 83, 92, 94, 97, 98, 100, 101, 105, 125, 128, 147, 148
Cobbs Island Hotel 95, 101
Cobbs Island Life-Saving Station 127
Cobb, T.L. 101
Cobb, Warren 93
Cobb-Wright Company 99
Coe's Out Neck 140
Coe, Timothy 140
Coldkill Creek 135
Colton, Mary-Russell Ferrell ii, 77, 78, 79, 80, 81
Commercial and Financial Chronicle 64
Concord Wharf 142, 147
Craddock Creek 141

Craddock Neck 141
Craddockville 141
Crawford 117
Crook, Abel 53, 54, 55
Crumb, C.H. 101
Crumb, Charles 127
Cushman, Caroline 105, 106
Cushman, Larimore H. 105, 106
Custis family 63, 110, 111
Custis, George Washington Parke 110
Custis, John 63, 104, 110
Custis Neck 159
Custis Tomb 150
Custis, William 62, 63

D

Dale's Gift 109, 154
Dale, Thomas 104, 154
Daugherty 159. See also Bull Run
Davidson, Thomas E. 7, 9, 10
Davis, L. Clarke 82, 86, 87, 88, 90, 91
Davis Wharf 141, 144, 147
Debdeavon 137
Delano, Chas. A. 56
Democratic Messenger 51, 96
Disston, Hamilton 43, 47, 48, 49, 50, 51
Disston, Henry 43, 47
Dixon, Thomas 148
Doughty family 69
Doughty, George 88, 89
Doughty, L.E. 67, 70, 84
Doughty, William J. 76
Downing's Oyster House 26
Downing, Thomas ii, 25, 26
Drummondtown 139, 146, 147
Dunton, Custis M. iii, 40
Dunton, J.R. 130, 133
Duryea, L.D. 56

E

Eastern Shore Barrier Islands Center 29, 67
Eastern Shore Herald 99
Eastern Shore Historical Society 29
Eastern Shore Indians of Virginia and Maryland 7
Eastern Shore Land Trust 166
Eastern Shore News 111, 112
Eastern Shore of Virginia National Wildlife Refuge 118, 119, 166
Eastern Shore of Virginia Produce Exchange 36
Eastern Shore Railroad 147
Eastern Shore Yacht and Country Club 140
Eastern Virginian 39, 40
Eastville 90, 91, 92, 138, 146, 147, 150
Eastville Inn 150
Egloff, Keith 8
Elliotts Neck 136
Elliott, Thomas G. 42, 160
Esk 128, 129, 130
Esk, Robert Montague 128
Ewing 117
Exmore ix, 69, 87, 89, 142
Eyre Hall 135
Eyreville Neck 135

F

Fairview Neck 141
Farmers' Register 18
Fell, George B. 59, 60
Ferrell, Elise Houston i, ii, vii, 75, 76, 77, 78, 80, 81, 82
Ferrell, Joseph L. i, ii, vii, 64, 75, 76, 77, 78, 80, 81, 82, 86, 87, 88, 90
Field, John W. 22, 23
Field, Samuel H. 23, 24
Finneys Creek 140, 159
Finneys Island 140
Finneys Neck 140
First People - The Early Indians of Virginia 8
Fisherman Inlet 126
Fisherman Island viii, 3, 108, 113, 114, 115, 117, 118, 119, 120, 121, 126, 128, 166
Fitchett, William and Margaret 92, 101
Flagler, Henry 49, 51, 65
Fletcher, Robert L. 36
Florence Killinger 126
flounder 1, 33
Folly Creek 34, 36, 56, 57, 139
Folly Creek Landing 35
Forest & Stream 42, 50, 73, 74, 160
Fort John Custis 118, 166
Fort Monroe 114, 115, 118
Fowler, Foote & Co 38
Franklin City ix, 21, 22, 148, 149
Franklin, John 21
Franktown 136, 146, 147, 158
Freeschool Neck 140
Fulton Fish Market vii, 28, 52, 55, 57

G

Gargaphia Neck 154
Gargatha Inlet 147
Garvis, Steve 103, 104
Gingerich, Joseph A.M. 13
Gingoteeks. See also Chincoteagues (tribe)
Godwin Island 58, 61
Goodwin, Richard H. 60
Great Depression viii, 57, 67, 92, 106
Great Neck 136
Great Sand Shoal Island 92, 101
Greenbackville 21
Greens Creek 10
Grosvenor, Gilbert 44
guano 22, 34, 36, 37, 38, 39, 128

Index

Guilford 140, 147
Guilford Creek 140, 155
Guilford Wharf 159

H

Hack family 140
Hacks Neck 140, 159
Hacks Neck and Its People, Past and Present 140
Hadlock 147
Hall, Richard F. Jr. 111, 112
Hall, Richard F. Sr. 111
Hamilton Disston (race horse) 51
Hampton 114
Hampton Roads 131
Hannibal 97
Harborton 38, 147, 159
Harper's New Monthly Magazine 149
Haxall Mills 97
H. Bossman 115
Henry Disston & Sons 43, 47
Henry Lee 97
Hitchins, George D. 110, 126
Hoffman's Wharf 147, 159. See also Harborton
Hog Creek 140
Hogg Island. See also Hog Island
Hog Island i, ii, iii, vi, vii, 4, 28, 29, 61, 64, 66, 67, 68, 69, 70, 71, 72, 73, 74, 75, 76, 77, 79, 81, 82, 83, 84, 86, 87, 88, 89, 90, 91, 123, 125, 128, 130, 131, 133, 140, 146, 147, 150
Hog Island Bay 136
Hog Island Virginia 67, 72
Hog Neck 140
Hog Neck Creek 140
Holden Creek 136, 140
Hollerith, Richard 59
Holmes Presbyterian Church 18
Holmes, Thompson 18, 19, 20, 70

Hope, Joanna Custis 62, 63
Horntown 146, 147
Hotel Wachapreague 34
Houston, Russell 75, 76
How the Word is Passed 26
Hungars Church 158
Hungars Creek 136, 143, 145, 155
Hunter, Alexander 70, 71, 72, 73, 74, 95, 96, 148
Hunting Creek 159
Hunting Wild Life with Camera and Flashlight 44, 45, 148
Hurley, George and Suzanne 111
Hutton, W.H.H. 116

I

In the Eastern Fluted Point Tradition 13
Island Neck 141

J

Jacobi, Herb 165
Jacobus Creek 136
James L. Day 156
James, Marinus 24
Jamestown 10, 104, 108, 109, 137, 153, 154, 155
Jamestown 117
Jamesville 142, 154
Jarvis, Samuel 90
Joanna 63
John and Francis 137
Johnson, John E. 131, 132, 133
Jollys Neck 136, 140
Jones, Tad 106, 107

K

Kailor, Robert 112
Kekotank Island 27
Kellam, Alfred S. 51, 53
Keller vii, 42, 51
Kimball, Sumner I. 124, 125, 127

177

King's Creek 135, 146, 154
Kiptopeke State Park 166
Kurlansky, Mark 26

L

Lang, Polk 36, 56, 57, 126
Lee, Mary Anne Randolph Custis 110
Lee, Robert E. 110
Lelandais, Pierre 112
Leonard Fish Company 15
Life and Death of the Salt Marsh 112
Lipford, Michael 163, 164
Little Hog Island 84
Little Machipongo Inlet 147
Little Mosquito Creek 136
Lloyd's Register of Shipping 99
Locust Mount 147
Locustville 147
Longboat Channel 1
Louisiana 157
Lyle gun 125, 131, 132

M

Machipongo 29, 68
Machipongo River 10, 40, 136
Magothy Bay 12, 62, 103, 153, 166
Manatee 43, 50
Mangum, Richard and Sherry 79, 80
Mappsburg 159
Mappsville 38
Marine Hospital Service 115, 116, 117
Mariner, Kirk 16, 17, 23, 24
Marionville 147
Mary Flagler Cary Charitable Trust 51, 61, 65, 164, 165, 166
Mattawoman Creek 136
Matthapunko Island. See also Hog Island
Mears, James Egbert 139, 140
Melfa 159

Messongo Creek 140
Messongo Neck 140
Metompkin Beach Hotel 36
Metompkin Inlet Coast Guard station 127
Metompkin Island 1, 33, 34, 61, 125, 127, 147, 165
midden 8, 11
migration 45, 120, 166
Migratory Bird Law 43
Migratory Bird Treaty Act vii, 43
Mitchell, Samuel A. 147
Mockhorn Island 4, 12, 13, 103, 104, 105, 107, 154
Modest Town 147
Morley's Wharf 141, 142, 144
Mosquito Creek 136
Muddy Creek 140
My Island Home 67
Myrtle Island 58, 61, 108, 109, 110, 111, 112, 147

N

Nandua Creek 140, 141, 145
NASA v, viii, 29, 30, 31, 136
Nassawadox ix, 155
Nassawadox Creek 136, 139, 141, 154
Nathan F. Cobb 98, 99, 100
Nathan F. Cobb and Sons Salvage Company 96, 97
National Geographic Magazine 43, 44, 47, 69
National Geographic Society 44, 148
Nelson, E.W. 46
Nelson, Francis 109
New Church 16, 139
Newport, Christopher 137
New York ii, vii, 11, 25, 26, 28, 42, 51, 52, 54, 55, 58, 59, 73, 87, 94, 98, 99, 105, 108, 111, 112, 124, 125, 130, 156, 157, 162, 164

New York City, New York ii, 26, 52, 55, 56, 148, 149
New York, Philadelphia and Norfolk (NYP&N) Railroad vii, 21, 42, 76, 139, 143, 147
New York Times 26, 49, 61
Noonan, Pat 61, 164, 165
Norfolk Gazette 99
Norfolk Landmark 89, 143
Norfolk, Virginia 37, 94, 97, 114, 115, 118, 126, 128, 129
Norfolk Virginian 115
Northampton-Accomack Memorial ix
Northampton County vi, ix, 10, 17, 18, 33, 62, 63, 64, 80, 90, 91, 92, 94, 103, 108, 110, 111, 112, 115, 135, 138, 139, 141, 142, 144, 146, 147, 153, 154, 166

O

Occohannock Creek 62, 141, 142, 143, 144, 145, 153
Occohannock Neck 136, 141, 142, 154
Occohannocks (tribe) 10
Ocean City Inlet 15
Old Dominion Gunning and Angling Association iii, 40, 41
Old Plantation Creek 109, 135, 143, 145, 159
Old Plantation Neck 135
Old Point Comfort 94
Old Town Neck 136
Oliphant, Charles 23, 24
Onancock 15, 30, 39, 40, 146, 167
Onancock Creek 33, 140, 145, 166, 167
Once Upon an Island 16, 23
One Woman's West 79
Onley 33
Outer Banks v, 83

Oyster 4, 67, 92, 98, 101, 103, 128

P

Painter 141
Panama 157
Panic of 1893 64, 82
Parkers Marsh 140
Parksley viii, 33
Parramore Beach 125, 127, 129
Parramore family 62, 63, 152
Parramore, George F. 54
Parramore Island iii, vii, 4, 28, 34, 40, 41, 52, 58, 59, 60, 61, 63, 64, 65, 78, 128, 129, 146, 165
Parramore, John 62, 63, 152, 153
Parramore Land and Improvement Company 64, 78, 80
Parramore, Thomas C. 62, 63, 159
Parramore, William 63
Parting Creek 136
Peninsula Enterprise 21, 23, 24, 35, 36, 38, 40, 41, 51, 53, 54, 55, 59, 99, 101, 115, 118, 126, 129, 136, 142
Pennsylvania i, vii, viii, 11, 19, 28, 29, 42, 43, 50, 51, 75, 81
Pennsylvania Railroad i, 28, 64, 76, 147
Perry, James R. 138
Pharsalia 18
Philadelphia, Pennsylvania 25, 29, 43, 47, 48, 50, 51, 64, 75, 76, 77, 78, 79, 88, 136, 147
Philadelphia Public Ledger 77, 87
Phoenix 109
Pickett's Harbor 166
Piney Island 14
Pitt's Creek 155
Pitt's Neck 140, 158
Pitt's Wharf 147
Plantation Creek 155
Pocomoke City 15

Pocomoke Creek 145
Pocomoke Neck 140
Pocomoke River 158
pony penning iii, 17, 18, 19, 20, 21, 22, 24, 27
Port of Baltimore 114
Pouliot, Richard and Julie 124, 125
Powell and Morse & Co 38
Powellton Hotel 51
Precious Memories of Childhood Days on Hog Island 67
Pungoteague 141, 146
Pungoteague Creek 140, 145, 155
Pyle, Howard 148, 149, 150, 151, 153

Q

Quinby 59
Quinby Inlet 41

R

railroad i, ii, vi, vii, viii, ix, 21, 36, 48, 49, 50, 51, 56, 64, 73, 75, 76, 82, 86, 94, 95, 135, 137, 141, 142, 143, 148, 149, 150, 157, 158, 159
Read's Wharf. See also Morley's Wharf
Red Bank 156, 160
Red Bank Creek viii, 145, 157
Red Bank Landing 66
Red Hills 33
Red Onion 67
Refuge Inn 15
Revell, John 40
Revels Island iii, vii, 4, 40, 41, 44, 45, 46, 50, 147, 148
Revels Island Bay 40
Revels Island Club iii, 40, 41, 42, 44, 45, 50
Revenue Cutter Service 98, 124, 127
Revenue Marine Bureau 124
Reverdly, Peter 104
Richmond Times-Dispatch 35

Richmond, Virginia 68, 90, 97, 164
Robert Koch 116, 117
Rogers, H.M. 56
Rountree, Helen C. 7, 9, 10
Rue's Wharf 142
Rue, William J. 142
Ruffin, Edmund 18

S

Salicornia 5
San Albano iii, 130, 131, 132, 133
Sandfordville. See also Sanford
Sand Hills 146
Sandy Island 4, 40, 41
Sandy Point 53
Sanford 147
Saunders, Jean 59
Savage, Asa 53, 127
Savage Creek 136, 138
Savage Neck 135, 137, 138
Savage Neck Dunes Natural Area Preserve 138
Savage, Thomas 137
Saxis 140
Scarburgh, Edmund 154
Scarburgh Neck 141
Schmidlapp, Carl 59, 60, 61
Schmidlapp family 59, 60, 61, 65
Scott, Benjamin Franklin 29, 30
Scribner's Monthly 149
Seashore Chronicles - Three Centuries of the Virginia Barrier Islands 73
Sea View 147
Selden 114, 116
Shady Side 147, 158
Shield's Wharf 142
Ship Shoal Island 58, 61, 108, 109, 111, 112, 147
Shipwrecks and Rescues Along the Barrier Islands of Delaware, Maryland, and Virginia 111

Index

Shipwrecks on the Virginia Coast 124
Shiras, George 3d vii, 42, 43, 44, 45, 46, 47, 50, 148
Shomette, Donald G. 97
Silver Beach 141
Simoneaston Bay 136
Simoneaston Creek 136
Sluitkill Neck 138, 140
Smith, Clint 26
Smith, Henry 114
Smith Island 3, 58, 61, 104, 105, 108, 109, 110, 111, 112, 125, 126, 128, 147, 154
Smith Island Development Corporation 58, 60, 64, 111, 112, 162
Smith Island Life-Saving Service 126
Smith, John 10, 109, 137
Smith's Beach 138
Smithsonian's National Museum of Natural History 12
spartina v, 3, 4, 5, 27, 135, 167
Spartina alterniflora 3, 5, 104
Spartina patens 5
Spratley, Henry M. 42, 56
Sterling, Charles A. 67, 68, 69, 71, 72, 73, 74, 123
Sterling, John E. 111
Stoner, Samuel L. 52, 55
Stout, Robert 29
Studies of the Virginia Eastern Shore in the 17th Century 152, 155
Sturgis, Joseph R. 89, 132, 133
Sunshine 87, 90
Swans Gut Creek 135

T

Tangier Island 38
Tanner, Henry S. 146, 147
Taylor Branch 141
Taylor Creek 140
Teal, John and Mildred 112

Teches Island. See also Parramore Island
The Auk 127
The Big Oyster - History on the Half Shell 26
The Eastern Shore - Maryland and Virginia 139
The End of an Era 144
The Formation of a Society on Virginia's Eastern Shore, 1615-1655 138
The Gulf. See also Savage Creek
The Horns. See also Eastville
The Huntsman in the South 71, 95, 148
The Isaacs 113
The Lost Colony (of North Carolina) 10, 68, 73
The Nature Conservancy 10, 51, 58, 59, 60, 61, 69, 101, 111, 128, 162, 163, 164, 165, 166, 167
The Sea Around Us 112
The Swash 41
Thomas Wharf 10, 11
Thoreau, Henry David 96
Tom's Cove 22, 23
Tom's Hook 15, 22, 39
Truitt, Barry R. 73, 110

U

Underground Railroad 26
University of Pennsylvania vii, 81, 82
Upshur Bay 40
Upshur, Ben 79
Upshur Creek 10
Upshur Neck 40, 91, 136
U.S. Coast Guard 98, 122, 127
U.S. Life-Saving Service iii, 93, 96, 97, 98, 99, 110, 116, 124, 127, 133
U.S. Lighthouse Board 73

V

Verrazano, Giovanni da 9, 108

Virginia Coast Reserve 61, 101, 163, 165
Virginia Master Naturalists 119
Virginia's Eastern Shore 28, 68, 104, 108

W

Wachapreague vii, 35, 36, 42, 43, 46, 50, 51, 52, 53, 55, 59, 91
Wachapreague Inlet 53
Wachapreague Literary Club 35, 127
Wachapreague wharf 35
Wallop, John 27, 28, 158
Wallops beach 31
Wallops Flight Facility 31, 136
Wallops Island v, viii, 20, 27, 30, 31, 125, 136, 147, 158
Wallops Island Association 28
Wallops Island Club viii, 28, 29
Wallops Island Life-Saving Station 127
Wallops Neck 136, 158
Wardtown 142, 147
Warehouse Prong 155
Washington, D.C. 41, 44, 73, 86, 118
Washington, George 110
Washington, Martha Dandridge Custis 104, 110
Washington News 117
Weir Point 33
Welburn, Thomas 16, 17
Wellington Neck 136, 158
West, Benjamin W. 52, 55
Whealton, John B. 127
Whitelaw, Ralph T. 28, 40, 62, 68, 69, 104, 108
Widgeon 21
Wigeon, Yvonne Marshall 67
William & Mary Center for Archaeological Research 10
Willis Wharf 67, 69, 84, 87, 90
Wilmington, Delaware 42, 87, 94, 148, 149, 151
Wilsonia Neck 136, 158
Wilsonia Wharf 147
Winders Neck 135
Wingert, C. W. 55
Wise, John S. 144, 146
Woodward, Deborah 8
Woodword 116
Worcester Railroad 147, 148
World War I viii, 118, 120
World War II viii, 30, 41, 59, 118, 120
wreckers 96, 97, 123
Wreck Island 59, 147

Y

yellow fever viii, 114
Yeo Neck 140

About the Author

CURTIS J. BADGER is a Delmarva native who grew up in Virginia, majored in English at Salisbury University and, with the exception of four years traveling as a U.S. Air Force photojournalist, has enjoyed a career photographing and writing about his native coast. His books include *Salt Tide: Cycles and Currents of Life Along the Coast*; *Bellevue Farm: Exploring Virginia's Coastal Countryside*; *A Natural History of Quiet Waters*; *The Wild Coast*; *Exploring Delmarva*; *A Culinary History of Delmarva*; and *Nathan Cobb's Island*, a children's book. He has won numerous awards for his writing and photography.

www.ingramcontent.com/pod-product-compliance
Lightning Source LLC
Chambersburg PA
CBHW070536170426
43200CB00011B/2440